trotman

Law

UNCOVERED

Careers Uncovered guides aim to expose the truth about what it's really like to work in a particular field, containing unusual and thought-provoking facts about the profession you are interested in. Written in a lively and accessible style, *Careers Uncovered* guides explore the highs and lows of the career, along with the job opportunities and skills and qualities you will need to help you make your way forward.

Titles in this series include:
Accountancy Uncovered
Art and Design Uncovered
Charity and Voluntary Work Uncovered
E-Commerce Uncovered
The Internet Uncovered
Journalism Uncovered, 2nd edition
Law Uncovered, 2nd edition
Marketing and PR Uncovered
Media Uncovered, 2nd edition
Medicine Uncovered, 2nd edition
Music Industry Uncovered, 2nd edition
Nursing and Midwifery Uncovered
Performing Arts Uncovered, 2nd edition
Sport and Fitness Uncovered, 2nd edition
Teaching Uncovered
The Travel Industry Uncovered
Working For Yourself Uncovered

trotman

MARGARET MCALPINE

Law

UNCOVERED

2nd edition

Law Uncovered

This second edition published in 2009 by Trotman Publishing,
a division of Crimson Publishing Ltd., Westminster House,
Kew Road, Richmond, Surrey TW9 2ND

© Trotman Publishing 2009

First edition published in 2003 by Trotman and Company Ltd

Author Margaret McAlpine

Revised by Gillian Sharp

British Library Cataloguing in Publication Data
A catalogue record for this book is available
from the British Library

ISBN 978 1 84455 173 6

Typeset by RefineCatch Ltd, Bungay, Suffolk

Printed and bound in Great Britain by
Athenaeum Press, Gateshead

CONTENTS

About The Authors

Margaret McAlpine taught for a number of years in schools and colleges in the Midlands and East Anglia before becoming a journalist. Today she writes for a variety of publications and has a particular interest in writing careers materials for young people.

Gill Sharp is a freelance careers adviser, trainer and writer.

CHAPTER 1

Myths and facts – a realistic look at a legal career

SO YOU'RE INTERESTED IN A LEGAL CAREER

Otherwise why would you have picked up this book?

Whether you're at school and considering your options, or already in work but thinking, vaguely, of a career change, something made you choose this book rather than one on accountancy, aromatherapy or beekeeping.

MAKING UP YOUR MIND

That's one thing this book will not do for you. What the following chapters aim to do is to help you to see a legal career for what it is – warts and all.

Law is an area of work that seems to have instant appeal, but immediate assumptions can be misleading. Take a moment to measure your views of law against reality.

THE IMAGE
Law – prestigious, respectable, high salaries, long lunches, justice for all.

THE REALITY
Law – top solicitors in 'City' firms *do* earn very good salaries, although there are more highly paid areas of work, such as finance and some sectors of information technology. However, long lunches are offset by lengthy working hours and the majority of non-City solicitors earn salaries which, while well above the national average, are comfortable rather than astronomical.

Most barristers are self-employed so their income can fluctuate dramatically. Junior barristers may find that they are actually earning much less than some of their classmates at university, while those at the zenith of the profession can command annual fees which are well into six figures.

Justice for all? That *is* the ideal, but the phrase is open to different perspectives and a lawyer's job is to obtain the best result for his or her client, based on sound research, interpretation of the evidence and clever arguments. So justice may not always be strictly served by the final outcome.

WHERE DO YOUR IDEAS COME FROM?
Television and films such as *Ally McBeal* and *Law and Order* have a great deal to answer for when it comes to stereotyping legal careers, whether they are based on police procedures, detective stories or the law profession itself. *Judge John Deed* is a recent British example, just one of many screen representations of lawyers on both sides of the Atlantic. They attract millions of viewers, but how realistic are they?

Disregarding the huge differences in how law is practised in Britain and the USA, all these programmes have a common theme. They show beautiful people tracking down villains and making sure that right prevails while carrying out tempestuous affairs and eating in expensive restaurants. Very few lawyers would recognise this as bearing any relationship to their own workstyle! For instance, most barristers and solicitors who specialise in criminal law deal with relatively minor offences, not high-profile murder cases.

A DOSE OF REALISM - A JOB IS A JOB

However prestigious or glamorous, all jobs have their downside. You may have to deal with a lot of routine paperwork, you could be frustrated by clients who don't follow your advice, or seeing a case go to a rival practice. Hopefully, these low points are outweighed by challenges, rewards and interesting work that has a positive conclusion.

You're going to spend something like 2000 hours a year at work over at least 30 years, so it's worth finding a career that you enjoy and which uses your particular talents. The majority of would-be lawyers are young people finishing school or taking undergraduate courses at university. Typically, they go straight into the profession by doing postgraduate legal study once they have completed their degrees – perhaps with a gap year in between. Where does this leave older people contemplating a career switch?

A CHANGE IS AS GOOD AS A REST

With determination, law can be a fulfilling later career choice. The Age Discrimination Act of 2006 has had a positive impact on the situation for older entrants and many legal firms welcome their experience, particularly if it is relevant to the area of law in which they wish to practise.

Case Study 1
Bridget Leach trained as a nurse. She left to raise her family but returned to nursing part-time. She decided to do a part-time Graduate Diploma in Law (GDL: a conversion course for those whose degree is in another subject), followed by the Legal Practice Course (LPC: which all intending solicitors must take).

Studying was much harder than I'd imagined, particularly as I was still doing agency nursing and running a home. There were a lot of facts to remember and the assignments came thick and fast. You couldn't afford to fall behind. But, on the whole, I found it fascinating, although I could have lived without some modules, such as solicitors accounts and land law. On the part-time programme, most of my fellow students

---

were also mature. I'm not sure how I would have coped with working alongside younger students. I might have felt they were faster or brighter, though I've since met people of my age who did the full-time course and they said that their life experience counter-balanced the fact that the 'youngsters' were sometimes quicker – but not necessarily right.

I came into law because I wanted to use my medical knowledge in a different way. Initially I intended to specialise in personal injury (PI) cases, but while I was still on the GDL, I became aware that there were also opportunities on the medical negligence side.

Finding work wasn't as hard as I imagined. I decided not to go for the very big London firms, because I didn't feel my qualifications were strong enough. I applied to several medium-sized firms who specialised in aspects of medical law – a growth area, with plenty of opportunities. I found that the interviewers were very interested in my hospital experience and it definitely went in my favour. I had several job offers and took this one because I wanted to represent clients who had suffered from medical mistakes and were seeking compensation. Some solicitors' practices act only for the health trusts themselves, but I wanted to help individuals who were often distressed and uncertain how to gain redress.

For anyone thinking of training or retraining, be prepared to find the going tough in terms of study and look for jobs where your previous career will stand you in good stead.

STILL INTERESTED IN A LEGAL CAREER? THEN START HERE . . .

The term 'legal career' covers a massive range of jobs so the first step is to think about your options.

Simply wanting a legal career is a good starting point, but, before committing yourself, a great deal of research is needed. Lawyers need to be skilled at finding out facts, digging deep, examining detail and analysing the evidence. Start now by pondering on the questions below.

- Do you see yourself as a barrister/advocate or a solicitor? (This is a major question. The two professions demand different skills and ways of working.)

- In what area of law do you want to specialise?

- Do you want to work in a particular region of the UK? Are you prepared to move to London or another major city?

- How are you going to finance your studies?

- Do you need to consider part-time courses that will allow you to earn some sort of income?

- Is earn-as-you-learn work-based training a more realistic option?

Once you start considering these questions, you will begin to flesh out a vague idea into an achievable strategy.

TRY BEFORE YOU BUY

Nobody buys a house without viewing it, or purchases a car without a test drive, so it would be a mistake to enter any profession without finding out what the work involves. In addition, work experience is important when you come to look for your first professional legal position.

HOW DO I FIND WORK EXPERIENCE?

Pick up the phone and ask. This might sound quite intimidating, but the direct approach is often the best. Or you could write to legal firms, explaining your ambitions and asking to spend some time with them. Be prepared to follow up with a phone call though, as they may not get back to you.

Some students have had success by calling into firms in person. Law student Martin Derc says: 'I polished up my CV, put on my best suit and went to several local solicitors' firms. I tried to meet a partner or the practice manger in person and spelled out what

I could do for them – which, at that point, was basic clerical duties. I think it definitely helped to look businesslike and sound keen. Two weeks' unpaid work experience eventually turned into a paid summer job. I continued to work for the firm in university vacations, doing much more responsible paralegal work. I'll get a good reference from them when I'm applying for training contracts. They have suggested that I come to them as a trainee, but I would prefer somewhere bigger. However, if I'm unsuccessful with the larger firms, it's certainly an option.'

If you're at school, college or university, careers tutors or careers/personal advisers should have some useful advice and practical leads.

Otherwise, personal contact is the way forward. If you have friends, family members or acquaintances who are working in law, do ask these people if they can help or suggest people for you to approach.

STILL UNSURE WHERE YOU'RE GOING?

Read on. Spend a few hours learning about legal careers and what they might offer you. Then you should be in a better position to start making decisions.

CHAPTER 2

What is law? How has it developed?

WHAT DIFFERENT LEGAL SYSTEMS EXIST?

Law is the set of rules by which countries are governed and society is regulated.

If people behaved exactly as they liked, there would be chaos, nobody would be safe and civilised society would collapse, which is why laws are required. The legal system gives a framework to these codes of behaviour, a system as to how they should be put into practice and a range of penalties for those who break the law.

THE BEGINNING

Laws were almost certainly in place from earliest times, long before they were written down. The invention of writing between about 3500 and 3000 BC meant laws could be recorded rather than remembered.

The first of such records appeared in the Middle East in Babylonia. The most famous Babylonian law code is that of King Hammurabi, which was drawn up in the 1700s BC. Around 1200 BC, the Israelites put their religious and social laws into a code, known as the Mosaic Code of Laws after the Israelite leader Moses.

It was the Ancient Greeks who decided human beings were capable of setting up their own laws and changing them when necessary. Athens' first code of law was drawn up by Drako in 621 BC. Unfortunately, his punishments were so harsh that his name lives on in the word 'draconian', meaning extremely severe. Luckily for the Athenians, around 80 years later a fairer code was drawn up.

WHEN IN ROME

The Laws of the Twelve Tables made up the first known Roman law code and remained the basis of Roman legal code, although they were adapted to meet changing circumstances. The only people able to interpret the huge number of Roman laws were the *juris prudentes* or experts in law. In modern English, the term jurisprudence means the science of law and it is a key subject in most law degrees. After the collapse of the Roman Empire, Roman law survived in the West as the basis for canon law – the law of the Roman Catholic Church. Around 1100 AD, the Italian university of Bologna started to train students from Italy and neighbouring countries in Roman law. Other universities followed their example and by the 1500s Roman law had been adopted throughout most of mainland Europe.

VIVE LA FRANCE

In order to centralise their government and increase their power, European kings tried hard to set up national legal codes for their countries. In 1800, Napoleon Bonaparte set up a committee to codify French civil law. The result was the Code Napoleon, which was so successful that it remains France's basic legal code today and became the model for civil law codes in most European countries, including Scotland – although not the rest of the UK.

1066 AND ALL THAT

By the time mainland Europe was developing Roman or civil law systems England had already developed its own legal system. Alfred the Great was the first ruler to establish equality under the law and by the time the Normans invaded in 1066, local courts were in operation across the country. The invaders retained these, but introduced a system of itinerant justices who were able to hear civil cases, which previously had to be taken to London. This became so popular that Henry II (1158–1189) divided England into circuits, setting up regular excursions from Westminster, a structure which lives on today. Out of the originally different legal customs across the country a process was developed known as common law because it was in common to England and, after the conquest of the Principality at the end of the thirteenth century, to Wales as well.

LEGAL FACTS

Before the merging of the two systems, an ancient law allowed the inhabitants of Hereford to kill Welsh people on a Sunday as long as they did it with a longbow in the cathedral close. On the other hand, the first known trial by jury was in Wales in the tenth century, long before Magna Carta enshrined it in English law.

AND THE REST IS HISTORY

Today in the UK there exist three major legal systems, each with its own legal rules, courts and legal professions.

ENGLAND AND WALES
This forms one jurisdiction or legal area. The national courts for England and Wales – the High Court, Court of Appeal and the House of Lords – are in London.

NORTHERN IRELAND
The legal system is similar in many ways to that of England and Wales (on which it was largely based) since the colonisation of the country in the seventeenth century. Some features do set it apart, however. These are often connected to the political instability and violence that have been part of life in the province since it was formed. For example, there are no juries in terrorist trials in Northern Ireland.

SCOTLAND
Scotland had developed its own system of laws and courts before it joined with England and Wales. The Acts of Union in 1707 allowed these to continue and Scottish law remains different from English law today.

Scottish firms have made inroads south of Hadrian's Wall, in the north-east of England and in London. Many aspects of Scottish law are very close to English legislation, for example employment regulations and judgments, and both jurisdictions are increasingly influenced by European law.

OFFSHORE

The Isle of Man and the Channel Islands are not governed by the British Parliament and have their own legal systems. Lawyers working in these locations often train on the mainland and qualify in English law, following this by gaining experience on the relevant island, before taking a further test in local legislation.

> **LEGAL FACTS**
>
> **Solicitors qualified in one of the four UK home countries wishing to work in a second region can take the Intra UK Transfer Test while lawyers from outside the UK take the Qualified Lawyers Transfer Test.**

DARE TO BE DIFFERENT

Today every independent country has its own legal system based on common law, civil law or a mixture of both. Most English-speaking countries, such as Australia and New Zealand, have systems founded on the common law system of England and Wales with certain variations for historical reasons.

As a result of its British heritage, the US system is based on common law, except for the state of Louisiana, which was colonised by the French and has a civil law system. Similarly Canada, a British dominion, has a common law system, except in the French-speaking province of Quebec, which bases its system on civil law.

After the collapse of communism in Eastern Europe in the early 1990s, the newly enfranchised countries, such as Romania, Poland and the Czech lands, asked for help in establishing revitalised legal systems. Many of these took English law as their foundation and lawyers from major British law firms travelled to the resurgent countries to give their input into the process.

EUROPEAN LAW

After the Second World War, countries in Western Europe began to work together in areas such as economics and defence. This led to the formation of the Council of Europe and of the North Atlantic Treaty Alliance (NATO) in 1949. Two years later, the Treaty of Paris expanded this co-operation. Today, membership of the European Community (EC) has increased to include more than 25 countries and it is still growing. Since 1972, when the UK signed the Treaty of Rome, the laws of the EC have in most cases been incorporated into UK law and, for the most part, member states adhere to the same basic precepts, such as in the area of human rights legislation. European law will continue to grow in importance and is an option on most UK law degrees. All EU countries have a reciprocal agreement whereby lawyers qualifying in one jurisdiction can move to another member state and practise there without supervision, once they have taken an examination on the laws prevailing there. Of course, in most instances, this means being fluent in the relevant language too. A more common method of working in Europe is to become a solicitor with a large English law firm which has bases or associate companies in cities such as Paris, Rome, Munich etc. The chances of being transferred to these locations, short term or long term, are high. Knowledge of the appropriate language will help, but may not always be necessary. Opportunities also exist in working for the EU institutions.

INTERNATIONAL LAW

We live in a global society with increasingly shared concerns about issues such as financial security, human rights, war and terrorism. So there has been a tremendous growth in legislation with a broad international focus, rather than a merely local application. Different countries collaborate on devising and developing laws that serve the widest possible community and this trend is likely to continue in the future.

WORKING ABROAD

Many UK-qualified lawyers want to work overseas. The simplest way to do this is the one referred to above under the European Law heading – find work in a top English legal practice with satellite offices, sister firms or clients in other parts of the world and apply for openings as they arise. These could be in Melbourne or Mumbai, the Middle East or Manchester, Manhattan or Munich. Moving permanently to a non-EU country is tricky, no matter how experienced you are. It is likely to be easier if you aim for somewhere like Australia, which is English-speaking, has various immigration schemes and a legal framework similar to our own, so that total requalification is not necessary, although you are likely to have to do some further training and be tested on this.

Remember that few countries outside the UK have a dual system of barristers/advocates and solicitors, so you may need to combine two different skill sets if you practise abroad.

The United States is a magnet for many people but, once again, the tried and trusted method of being employed by a UK firm with a presence in North America is still the best method of finding a foothold there. There is also a smattering of US law companies based in London, who recruit British-trained lawyers; competition for such posts is fierce, but the potential for travel across the Atlantic is high. Why not just take a job in the USA? First and foremost, work permits are hard to come by. Secondly, like other big countries such as Australia and Canada, the different states have their own Bar examinations which foreign lawyers must pass. Finally, although it is possible to do exams for the New York Bar through colleges in the UK, this is expensive and in no way guarantees a job in the Big Apple because US citizens are always given preference over incomers.

CHAPTER 3

A legal quiz — how much do you know?

Before reading further, it's time to find out how much you know about a legal career.

QUESTIONS

1. You don't need a law degree if you want to follow a legal career in the UK.
   True ☐ false ☐ or partly true ☐

2. Only barristers can speak in court.
   True ☐ false ☐ or partly true ☐

3. There are more men than women in the UK legal profession and minority groups are under-represented.
   True ☐ false ☐ or partly true ☐

4. Who is a fee-earner?

5. Any qualification that has an element of law in it brings exemption from some aspect of legal training.
    True ☐ false ☐ or partly true ☐

6. It's better to do a law degree than take another subject as an undergraduate and then do a conversion course.
    True ☐ false ☐ or partly true ☐

7. How many 'core' subjects, known as foundations of legal knowledge, are there in a law degree or conversion course?

8. You need a degree from a top-ranking university in order to find work in the law.
    True ☐ false ☐ or partly true ☐

9. You need at least a 2:1 at degree level in order to find work as a lawyer.
    True ☐ false ☐ or partly true ☐

10. What is intellectual property?

ANSWERS

1. **PARTLY TRUE** The choice is yours as to whether to take a law or non-law degree, although the latter route is less common in Scotland and Northern Ireland. Many solicitors and barristers have studied other subjects as undergraduates. Of these, the majority are in arts, languages and humanities subjects, but you can and do find lawyers with backgrounds in science and creative/performing arts. Many legal employers value the extra dimension that a non-law qualification can provide. In addition, some solicitors in England and Wales have qualified via the Institute of Legal Executives (ILEX) route, which is equivalent to a law degree but is taken while working (see Chapter 5).

2. **FALSE** Solicitors in England and Wales have always been able to speak or have right of audience, as it is known, in magistrates' courts, county courts and in crown courts at an appeal or a sentencing committed from a magistrates' court.

Since 1993, solicitors have been able to obtain full right of audience in the High Court, Crown Court, Court of Appeal and House of Lords after undergoing training and gaining an advocacy certificate. Relatively few solicitors have so far taken advantage of this opportunity. Legal executives are also hoping to gain full rights of audience in the future. However, these increased advocacy rights are an important step in blurring the differences between barristers and solicitors and raise the question of whether one day the two professions will merge.

3. **FALSE** Times are definitely changing. For instance, today there are more women graduates with 1st and 2:1 class law degrees than men. In England and Wales, the number of women solicitors has more than doubled since the 1990s. In 2007, women accounted for 43.7 per cent of solicitors with practising certificates. 62.7 per cent of students currently enrolled with the Law Society are women and 30.7 per cent are from ethnic minority groups. These trends have also affected the Bar. Now 20 per cent of pupils, 10 per cent of barristers and five per cent of Queen's Counsels (QC) declare themselves to be 'non white'. It remains tough for women to become senior barristers, but they are making steady inroads into the profession as a whole and the number of female QCs will rise over the next few years.

In terms of age, many barristers' chambers and numerous law firms have always welcomed older applicants. The Age Discrimination Act of 2006 has increased this trend, although some mature students still feel they have to work harder to secure an interview and a training place than their younger classmates.

Perhaps the biggest barrier to success is not gender, race or age, but academic achievement: see the answer to question 9 for a fuller explanation.

Both the Law Society and the Bar Council are committed to equal opportunities and have staff to monitor this. Scottish and Northern Irish professional bodies also support equality and diversity.

4. **FEE EARNER** A fee earner is highly prized by his or her employers as a legal professional who can bill clients for a set amount of money for specific tasks. So most solicitors are fee earners as their firm charges out their time (typically in blocks of 15 minutes) at a particular rate depending on seniority, duties undertaken and type of case. Many legal executives and some paralegals are also fee earners.

5. **PARTLY TRUE** For instance, the ILEX exams grant exemption from courses such as the LPC, depending on what level has been reached. A qualifying law degree also means that there is no need to do a conversion scheme before going on to the LPC. It's worth bearing in mind here that not all law degrees are regarded as 'qualifying' by the Law Society, so be sure to check this before committing yourself to an undergraduate programme. However, postgraduate courses with purely academic content such as Master's courses (LLMs) and PhDs will not give any extra benefit in terms of cutting down on practical training for any law-related job.

6. **FALSE** 'Better' is a highly subjective term. In the sense that it lops a year off your practical training, a law degree could be seen as advantageous. However, some students report that they found such a concentrated focus on just one subject quite limiting and would have preferred to study something else for its own sake. One way round this is to do a qualifying law degree with another minor subject. If this is a language you may be able to obtain some kind of law qualification from another country during your year abroad. Those who have taken a non-law degree seem generally satisfied with this route, although they admit that the conversion qualification is very intense – and can be expensive.

7. **CORE SUBJECTS** Public law, law of the European Union, criminal law, obligations (which includes tort, contract and restitution), property law, and equity and trusts. If you take a conversion course such as the GDL then these will form the bulk of your studies. If you do a law degree instead, you will be able to slot in additional options and specialist studies in other legal areas that interest you.

8. **FALSE**   For instance, less than 20 per cent of pupil (newly qualified) barristers are from Oxford or Cambridge. The remainder come from a wide spread of universities. While there may still be a tendency for certain chambers to opt for graduates from the older, more traditional universities, the Bar is far more egalitarian now than it was even 10 years ago and so are top solicitors' firms. Red brick and 'new' universities are well represented in both areas.

9. **PARTLY TRUE**   A 2:1 is definitely a help, especially when applying for the Bar or for big City solicitors' practices. A 2:2 or lower may exclude you from some of these training opportunities and, increasingly, smaller legal firms may say that they prefer a 2:1. However, many firms will consider those with 2:2s and/or will take into account any extenuating circumstances. Relevant experience may also mitigate in your favour if you are in this situation.

10. **INTELLECTUAL PROPERTY (IP)**   IP is nothing to do with selling houses, but is very much a growing legal specialism. It is concerned with who owns the rights to items such as patents, titles, designs, published works and ideas. More recently it has covered disputes over internet domains and websites. It is just one example of how the law is evolving and developing to cover new areas as society changes.

What was your score? If some of the answers surprised you, it just goes to show that there are lots of myths surrounding the legal profession and that it has increasingly moved with the times. Nonetheless, it's still important to be practical, objective and self-aware when considering a law career, to evaluate the type and nature of study that you could do, and to choose a route and a legal niche that suits you.

Read on to find out about whether the law is right for you and, just as important, are you right for the law?

CHAPTER 4

Is a legal career right for you? Are you right for a legal career?

You want a challenge? Qualifying as a lawyer is certainly a challenge in itself and then there are further hurdles ahead.

GOING THROUGH THE HOOPS

1   EDUCATION

There are a range of academic hurdles to overcome before you even start your career. If you decide to go down the law-degree route, gaining a place on a course is an achievement in itself. Typical offers from universities offering a qualifying law degree are A level grades of AAB/ABB and Scottish Highers AAAAB/ABBBB. It is possible to get in with lower grades, but this may restrict your options when you are eventually looking for work. Many employers do take A level and equivalent results into account when deciding whether to interview trainee solicitors or pupil barristers/would-be advocates.

Qualifying in the jurisdiction of England and Wales and, to some extent, Scotland and Northern Ireland, allows you to choose a non-law degree if you wish. You will then have to take a further year of study – or two years if you opt for a part-time programme.

This stage is followed in England and Wales by either the LPC (for solicitors in England and Wales) or the Bar Vocational Course (BVC) for intending barristers. In Scotland and Northern Ireland, prospective lawyers combine practical training with study in a slightly different way. More will be explained in Chapters 5 and 7.

At all points, academic results are important and will be taken into account by recruiters.

2   TRAINING IN ENGLAND AND WALES

Only after you've been through all of the above do you begin your professional training within a working context. For solicitors, this means a two-year training contract. You straddle two worlds; earning a salary and learning at the same time. By assisting in a range of different departments or 'seats', you gain a good overview of where your strengths and interests lie.

Barristers need to take up pupillages – places in chambers where they help out more experienced barristers and take on minor cases of their own – for two years. As Chapter 8 will explain, finding a pupillage is not straightforward and many applicants are disappointed and have to look for other sorts of legal work at this point.

This stage is very competitive: not everyone who completes a legal education manages to obtain a training contract, pupillage or similar opportunity.

3   SPECIALISATION

Most qualified and experienced lawyers do specialise to some degree – less so in smaller solicitors' practices. They have to keep up with their subject and general developments in law by reading, attending conferences and undertaking mandatory Continuing Professional Development (CPD). Some may choose to take on extra responsibilities within their organisation – for instance the training of junior staff – or outside the firm. For example, a family lawyer may decide to become a member of the local panel that reviews childcare proceedings. Solicitors in private practice often aspire to being partners; this means taking a share of the profits, but also being accountable for the successful running of the firm. For barristers, most of whom are self-employed, the imperative is to build up a reputation and generate sufficient work to make a good living.

All of this has to be done alongside the day-to-day business of working with clients, so multi-tasking is a necessity, not an option.

WHAT DOES A LEGAL CAREER MEAN?

Case Study 2
Common to both branches of law is the hard work involved. Paul Matthews is a trainee solicitor in a major city firm.

Once I found my training contract, I thought that I'd reached my goal. Instead I quickly realised that I'd only just begun. Applying my knowledge to real cases is fun but testing and sometimes stressful. Sometimes clients are difficult – and law school doesn't really give you any experience of that – and dealing with several demanding cases at the same time is tiring. I often work late: 9–5 is a concept rather than a reality for most junior solicitors. I didn't like one of my seats (property), but I just had to grin and bear it, knowing that it would be over in a few months. Despite everything, I really enjoy the work and get a huge buzz when we achieve a result for a client.

Case Study 3
Rose Richards is a partner in a solicitors' firm and specialises in insurance and pensions.

It's clichéd but true to say that every day is different. I can go into the office one morning thinking that I've cracked a case and then some new details will emerge and more work needs doing! I love the research side so this is fine by me. But deadlines have to be met, so one can't always indulge in what one likes. I started my career in a City law practice and left to come to a smaller niche firm outside London because I didn't like the lifestyle or the pressure. It's good to build up some standing in a particular branch of law. Running the firm brings good financial rewards, but the nitty gritty of managing staff can eat into the strictly legal side of the job. There are upsides – I travel a lot, as far afield as Singapore and Australia and last year I had to do a presentation at a big conference in the south of France, though I had no time to spend on the beach! Likewise there are downsides – I often take work home and can't spend as much time with my daughters as I would wish.

WHAT MAKES A GOOD LAWYER?

Remember that gaining the grades to study law is not sufficient reason for opting for a legal career. Personal motivation and determination are needed and, while academic aptitude is important, it should be accompanied by specific qualities and skills:

- a fascination for the law itself – how it works, how it changes, how it can be interpreted

- a rational approach to the subject and pleasure in discovering the reasoning behind a legal decision

- creative thinking – an ability to look at situations from a new angle or a fresh perspective

- confidence to discuss matters verbally and to make points clearly

- ability to get on well with people from different backgrounds

- attention to detail

- a liking for people and the personality to work with them objectively and sympathetically

- capacity to digest large amounts of information and pick out key points

- good writing skills

- ability to work long hours and deal with a heavy workload

- team work – satisfaction and stimulation in co-operating with colleagues

- strong personal organisational skills.

If you recognise yourself in this list of qualities then a legal career could be right for you. But remember this book is only a starting point. Do your homework, gain experience and talk to people. Wrong decisions can be expensive and demoralising. Find out as much as you can about different courses, training opportunities and aspects of legal work before taking action.

CHAPTER 5

A career as a solicitor — what exactly do solicitors do?

Most readers of this book will visit solicitors only when they want to make a will, buy a house, split up with a partner or (possibly) when they have been charged with a criminal offence. However, solicitors' duties are far wider than this. Their clients are usually members of the public or business people who need advice on legal matters, disputes and financial transactions. Solicitors represent clients in magistrates' courts and county courts. More serious criminal cases are heard in the Crown Court where a solicitor will normally brief a barrister to speak on behalf of a client.

Clearly, a solicitor's job can vary according to specialisation and location; working in a large city with business clients can be very different to operating from a smaller town or high-street practice. Legal aid work (subsidised by the government to provide legal help for those who may not otherwise be able to access or afford it) is obviously different again, as is being part of a niche practice focusing on a specific area of law, for example media or shipping. So there is plenty of chance to follow your own interests, but there are certain functions and duties common to all solicitors:

- contact with clients face to face, over the phone and by email and letter (Barristers and advocates have much less opportunity for this and it is one of the key differences between the two professions.)

- liaison with other legal professionals and outside agencies, from financial institutions to police and social workers

- researching complex facts and regulations and interpreting these for clients

- drafting and writing reports and correspondence, often in great detail

- managing cases and caseloads

- contributing to colleagues' work as part of a team, but also working independently towards a common goal.

There is a growing tendency for solicitors to specialise in a particular area of legal work, such as:

- business and commercial law

- property

- corporate, partnership and insolvency (together the above are known as Chancery)

- probate (sorting out wills and bequests)

- litigation (advising clients over disputes and disagreements)

- criminal law (crimes or public wrongs punishable by the state – such as manslaughter, robbery or fraud). It's important to bear in mind that most criminal cases are low level – taking and driving away, for instance – rather than headline-grabbing murders or mayhem

- family law – divorce proceedings, childcare agreements etc

- civil law (disputes between individuals or businesses over issues such as personal injury or negligence)

- environmental law – dealing with issues such as emissions and trading advice

- employment law

- European law – the most usual areas being competition law, employment law and human rights.

This is quite a basic list of the most common specialisms. There is an ever-growing list of niche areas, most of them offered by the larger corporate firms. Civil liberties and sports law are just two examples of fields which have developed in the recent past, but there's something for everyone if you delve deep enough – including such esoteric subjects as space law. Publications such as *The Legal 500* and the *Chambers Directory* give an excellent overview of what is available.

WHERE DO SOLICITORS WORK?

PRIVATE PRACTICE
About 80 per cent of solicitors work in private practice. The size of these varies from sole practitioners and small firms on the high street, to larger local chains and medium-sized companies, up to huge legal firms employing vast numbers of lawyers.

Although the vast majority of solicitors work in private practice, there are good employment opportunities in other areas, as described below.

CROWN PROSECUTION SERVICE AND CROWN OFFICE AND PROCURATOR FISCAL SERVICE
Since 1985 criminal prosecutions have been undertaken by the Crown Prosecution Service (CPS), or Crown Office and Procurator Fiscal Service in Scotland (COPFS), while the defence is carried out by lawyers in private practice.

To give some idea of the scale of this work, the CPS prosecutes in court around 1.5 million cases every year. In order for a case to be brought to court, CPS/COPFS lawyers must consider that there is good chance of securing a conviction. Solicitors in the CPS will make an assessment and advise the police on whether there is enough evidence to bring a prosecution case. When sufficient evidence is available, they carry out the pre-court preparation work as well as playing their part in the court proceedings.

GOVERNMENT

There are three main types of government work.

- advising ministers and administrators on the law and the way in which it affects their departments

- drafting and framing new legislation

- carrying out many of the tasks undertaken by solicitors in private practice for people who are under age or for physical or mental reasons are unable to represent themselves.

Work in the Government Legal Service tends to be less well paid than private practice. None the less, it brings with it the chance to move from department to department and experience a variety of work, plus the chance to be involved in serious issues – often at the cutting edge of law – early in your career.

LOCAL AUTHORITIES

Lawyers are employed by county councils, borough councils and district councils to give legal advice on issues affecting local government. These can be wide ranging, covering routine matters as well as those that have a wider impact. The legal team might deal with childcare, licensing applications, planning, environmental concerns, employment disputes and anything that affects the local population, the council's workforce and the provision of amenities.

INDUSTRY AND COMMERCE

Large organisations, including banks, insurance firms, utility companies, manufacturing and commercial operations, often have their own in-house legal departments to look after their interests.

PAY

After completion of training and especially once they have two years' post-qualifying experience, solicitors can earn well above the national average. Again, it can vary according to area, specialisation and size of firm. It is not unrealistic for a solicitor who has just finished their training contract in a small regional firm to earn £30 000 plus, slightly less in some high-street practices and substantially more for those based in a big firm in a major city. In fact, in some London legal concerns, newly qualified solicitors earn over £60 000 straight after completing their training contracts. With more experience, this can rise dramatically: even in very small practices an annual figure of £60 000–75 000 is not unrealistic. Becoming a partner will usually involve a six-figure salary, which, again soars to a higher level in the biggest firms. Work in the courts service and local/central government departments will provide a comfortable salary but it may not reach the giddy heights of private practice. As a rule of thumb, the worst paid areas tend to be those specialising in social justice (legal aid, human rights etc) or crime, though most solicitors in these fields are not driven by financial reward.

TRAINING TO BE A SOLICITOR IN ENGLAND AND WALES

At the time of writing, there are two stages of training. It was recently suggested by the Solicitors Regulation Authority that the current two-year training contract could be more flexible and that the contract itself could be replaced by less formal arrangements and work-based learning. This alternative was piloted in 2008. It remains to be seen how legal firms themselves respond to these ideas. Quite possibly any new system might exist side by side with the traditional pattern and it would be up to employers to decide which they preferred.

The academic stage – this is obtained by following:

● the law-degree route, or

● the non-law degree route (England and Wales only), or

● the ILEX route (England and Wales only).

The vocational stage – this is obtained by:

- completion of the LPC

- followed by a two-year training contract.

FIGURE 1: TRAINING AS A SOLICITOR IN ENGLAND AND WALES

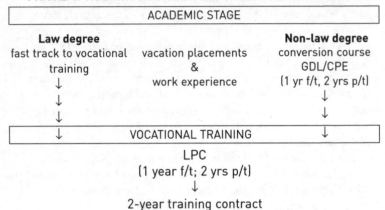

ACADEMIC STAGE		
Law degree		**Non-law degree**
fast track to vocational	vacation placements	conversion course
training	&	GDL/CPE
↓	work experience	(1 yr f/t, 2 yrs p/t)
↓		↓
↓		↓

↓	VOCATIONAL TRAINING	↓

LPC
(1 year f/t; 2 yrs p/t)
↓
2-year training contract

THE LAW DEGREE ROUTE

> **LEGAL FACT**
>
> **There is one university in England and Wales which offers a four-year qualifying law degree with an integrated qualification, exempting students from the LPC or the BVC. For more details see the website of the University of Northumbria (www.northumbria.ac.uk).**

The most popular mode of study is to take a law degree that is recognised as a qualifying law degree by the Law Society. No particular A level subjects are required for a place on a law course and science subjects are as acceptable as arts subjects. However, competition for places is strong. Typical offers from universities ask for A level grades of AAB/ABB and for Scottish Highers AAAAB/ABBBB.

It is vital to make sure that the course you choose is recognised as covering the foundations of legal knowledge as required by the

Law Society and the General Council for the Bar. Most university prospectuses which offer a qualifying law degree will state this clearly in their prospectus. If in any doubt, check with the college itself or the Law Society.

ADVANTAGES OF THE LAW DEGREE ROUTE

This is the quickest way to qualify because, having graduated, you can proceed straight to the vocational stage of training. Also, if you like getting to grips with detail and pursuing some specialist legal interests, it can be very satisfying. Emma Robson, a trainee solicitor, comments: 'I was able to do my dissertation on an area of EU law that particularly fascinated me and I'm sure that helped me to get a training contract.'

DISADVANTAGES OF THE LAW DEGREE ROUTE

It means narrowing your study options at an early stage.

Stephen James is a solicitor who did a law degree. He says: 'With hindsight, I would have preferred to have taken another academic subject for sheer enjoyment, so studying it for three years was a slog. I found a lot of the degree quite dry and boring – and I don't use half of it in my job.'

THE NON-LAW DEGREE ROUTE

THE COMMON PROFESSIONAL EXAMINATION/ GRADUATE DIPLOMA IN LAW

Graduates with a 1st degree (BA or BSc) in any subject or a non-qualifying law degree can take a conversion course. In England and Wales, this leads to the Graduate Diploma in Law or GDL (still sometimes referred to by its older name of Common Professional Examination (CPE)). It enables students to complete the academic stage of training by covering the foundation subjects that underpin law over one year full-time, two years part-time, or via distance learning. It can be tough going because you are cramming the main content of a law degree into a very short period of time!

A list of courses can be found on the Law Society website. Apply for full-time courses via the Central Applications Board (see Useful Addresses). For part-time study, apply to the institution itself. After the successful completion of a GDL/CPE you can go on to an LPC in the same way as a graduate with a law degree.

ADVANTAGES OF THE NON-LAW DEGREE ROUTE

You keep your study options open longer and you have the opportunity to study any academic subject to degree level. For some people, a first degree in another subject can enhance their chances if the topic is relevant to the type of law that they want to practise. There is a point of view that some law firms may be uncertain about degrees such as art or music. In this case, it would be up to the graduates concerned to market their background proactively and positively: it has been done successfully in many instances.

DISADVANTAGES OF THE NON-LAW DEGREE ROUTE

You're studying for longer and face the cost of an additional year's study. Fees for the GDL course are between £3000 and £7000. You also need to consider living expenses during this period although part-time or distance learning can be combined with a job.

THE VOCATIONAL STAGE

Once the academic stage is completed, students move on to the vocational stage.

The first stage of vocational training is the LPC, which is one year full-time and two years part-time and is run at institutions across the country.

LEGAL PRACTICE COURSE

This comprises a mixture of written examinations, accounts and skills assessments. Amongst other subjects, you will cover:

- compulsory or core practice areas – these include business law and practice, litigation (civil and criminal), property law and practice

- legal skills – these include advocacy, interviewing and advising, legal writing and drafting, practical legal research, problem-solving and IT

- pervasive areas – these include topics such as professional conduct and regulations, wills and administration, taxation

- elective areas – students have to study three electives from a very wide range of subjects. The choice of these is often based around the type of work to be undertaken during the training contract, for example if you want to work in the City, you would be advised to take corporate options.

You need to apply for a place on an LPC course early and ideally by December of the year before you want to start the course. Online application forms are available through the Central Applications Board (see Useful Addresses). In the case of a part-time course, you apply directly to the college. A list of recognised courses can be found on the Law Society website.

THE TRAINING CONTRACT

Having reached this point in your career you face yet another hurdle – finding a training contract.

This means that you are attached to a firm of qualified solicitors, or another authorised training establishment, for two years. Their role is to advise and guide you while monitoring your progress, giving you a range of work, introducing you to new areas of law, and paying you a salary. In 2007, the minimum starting pay for trainee solicitors outside London was £15 280 (£17 600 for those in the capital), which rises quite rapidly as the trainee progresses through the contract and becomes more experienced. This basic amount is most likely to be paid to someone starting out in a small high-street practice. Some larger firms can be more generous and in the big City firms, a few talented trainees may begin their career on £30 000-plus. On the other hand, as one City trainee commented, 'They want blood!', that is, long hours and extremely hard work are the order of the day.

No amount of academic qualifications will guarantee you a training contract. Figures suggest that up to 20 per cent of applicants are disappointed. In order to be one of those who aren't, you need to do your research and market yourself as strongly as possible. See Chapter 7 for advice on gaining a training contract.

During your training-contract period you need to complete the Professional Skills Course. This is divided into five modules that build on the three key subject areas of the LPC:

- finance and business skills

- advocacy and communication skills

- client care and professional standards.

On successful completion of a training contract you can pat yourself on the back and apply to the Law Society for admission as a solicitor.

THE ILEX ROUTE
You can become a solicitor without having a degree by following the Institute of Legal Executives or legal training route. Training is usually carried out on a part-time basis while working with a legal firm, although some colleges do run full-time courses and ILEX itself provides distance learning courses.

QUALIFYING AS A LEGAL EXECUTIVE
The minimum educational requirements are:

- four GCSE passes at grades A–C in academic subjects including English, although many legal executives do have A levels or the equivalent.

Mature students over the age of 25 years without formal qualifications may be considered on the basis of their legal, business, commercial, academic or other experience.

To become a Member of the Institute of Legal Executives (MInstLEx) you need to pass the membership examinations, which are set in two stages.

The Level 3 Professional Diploma in Law is usually taken over two years. It is set at A level standard and covers most of the areas of law and legal practice encountered in the legal profession. There are two routes:

- examination route – consisting of four papers covering the English legal system and essential elements of law and practice

- mixed assessment route – including a portfolio, case studies and one end-of-course examination.

Learning is usually part-time at a local college or by home study.

The Level 6 (previously Level 4) Professional Higher Diploma in Law is usually taken over two years and is set at degree level. One area that it covers is specialist practice which ties in with the actual day-to-day work being done by the candidate.

The majority of trainee legal executives complete the membership examinations over a four-year period taking two papers a year. You don't need to have any legal employment experience to achieve membership status, but it *is* necessary to achieve fellowship status.

In order to qualify as a fellow (FInstLEx) you need to:

● be over 25 years of age

● be a member of the Institute of Legal Executives

● have completed five years' qualifying legal experience of which two years must have been completed after achieving ILEX Professional Diploma in Law Status.

QUALIFYING AS A SOLICITOR

The academic stage
As a legal executive wishing to qualify as a solicitor you need either to pass the GDL (or CPE) or claim exemption by having passed corresponding papers in the ILEX Professional Higher Diploma in law Level 4 examination.

The vocational stage
To complete this stage of training, legal executives must:

● be enrolled as a student member of the Law Society

● complete the LPC

● complete or be exempt from a two-year training contract

● complete the Professional Skills Course.

The LPC

Before starting this course, legal executives must:

- be a MInstLEx

- have served three years' qualifying employment after the age of 18

- have been granted exemption from or completed the GDL/CPE

- be a student member of the Law Society

- have been granted a certificate of completion of the academic stage

or

- be a FInstLEx and meet the above requirements with the exception of the qualifying employment period.

THE ILEX ROUTE FOR LAW GRADUATES

Legal executives who have a recognised law degree are exempted from Level 3 examinations, but still have to take Level 6; the Graduate Entry Diploma is an alternative way for such staff to qualify for ILEX membership and fellowship and then to train as solicitors if they wish. Law graduates who have a qualifying law degree recognised by the Law Society, and who graduated within the last seven years, may apply to be exempt from the academic part of the ILEX qualification. They may still have to pass examinations in legal practice, usually by studying part-time while working full-time in a solicitor's office or legal department.

TRAINING CONTRACT

Fellows can claim exemption from the training contract, with certain provisos. Members must complete the LPC and a two-year training contract. The Professional Skills Course is mandatory for everyone.

ADVANTAGES OF THE ILEX ROUTE

You're in employment and you don't have to deal with the massive costs involved in degree and postgraduate courses.

DISADVANTAGES OF THE ILEX ROUTE
Achieving solicitor status by this route does take a long time.

Case Study 4
Gill Morgan is a legal executive who qualified as a solicitor and who is now a partner in her own firm in the west of England.

I originally worked in a high-street practice, which means I dealt largely with wills and probate, conveyancing, divorce and matters arising from it, general commercial issues and minor criminal offences,

I left school at 16 with the equivalent of five GCSEs – I was definitely not academic. I started out as a glorified office junior in a solicitors' firm and loved it from the start. My boss asked me if I wanted to become a legal executive and they sponsored me through the course. I won't say that I enjoyed it exactly but it was bearable, mainly because it tied in with what I was doing anyway. And I realised that it could lead to greater things!

After I took my ILEX exams, I stayed in the firm and built up the necessary experience so it seemed silly not to get the solicitors' qualification. It wasn't something I'd thought about at age 16, but by then I was in my 20s and wanted a career.

I studied at evening class – and in my own time, of course. It was a slog on top of a busy job, but worth it.

After working for someone else for so long, I hankered after running my own business and set up with two former colleagues several years ago. We're a high-street firm in a small country town and we're doing pretty well. There's a lot of variety in a practice like this and I feel as if I'm serving the community.

QUALIFYING AS A SOLICITOR IN OTHER BRITISH JURISDICTIONS

As noted in Chapter 2, the legal system and legal training in Scotland, Northern Ireland and the offshore islands is different to that of England and Wales. The other two Celtic countries operate a dual system of solicitors and barristers, while a 'fused' system operates in the Isle of Man and the Channel Islands. There, lawyers are known as advocates, although this is sometimes subdivided into solicitors and barristers. However, a lot of what has already been said in this chapter and in the preceding one also applies here in terms of skills, nature of the work, specialist possibilities, different workplaces and the skills and qualities needed. So if you are a reader outside England and Wales, don't ignore the preceding pages!

SCOTLAND

Routes to qualification as a solicitor are through an approved law degree (normally an LLB) course offered at 10 Scottish universities, followed by the six-month Diploma in Legal Practice and a two-year training contract. Entry to the diploma is highly competitive, with many more candidates than there are places and your Higher and undergraduate grades *will* count! Those without a law degree can undertake a three-year traineeship in a solicitor's office and sit the Law Society of Scotland's examinations, prior to taking the Diploma. The Diploma is run at five institutions and the deadline for applications is usually around Easter. It is a practically orientated course, covering:

● civil court practice

● criminal court practice

● private clients

● financial and related services

● accountancy

● professional responsibility

● and options in company/commercial law or public administration.

Securing a training contract is as competitive as it is in England and Wales and follows similar aims and patterns.

Alternatively, graduates with a degree in a subject other than law may be able to take an accelerated law degree course and gain an ordinary degree in two years and an Honours degree in three years.

LEGAL FACT

Dundee is the only university in Scotland that offers a degree in English law.

NORTHERN IRELAND

A law degree is the most usual prerequisite. Two universities (Queen's Belfast and Ulster) have law schools and some law degrees from England, Wales and the Republic of Ireland are also acceptable. Unlike the other UK countries, the practical and vocational phases of training overlap.

Solicitor training is known as apprenticeship and involves work in a solicitor's office under a master who is a qualified solicitor. An initial period of four months' work experience is followed by a year's full-time study for the Certificate in Professional Legal Studies, also taken by intending barristers. The trainee then returns to the office for the final eight months of training.

Graduates with a degree in a subject other than law need to show the Law Society of Northern Ireland that they have a satisfactory level of legal knowledge. The way to do this is by taking the Bachelor of Legal Science conversion course at Queen's University Belfast, full-time or part-time. Finally, anyone over the age of 29 who has been employed in a solicitor's practice for seven years and can satisfy the Law Society of Northern Ireland that he or she has gained the necessary knowledge and experience can also begin training as a solicitor.

THE CHANNEL ISLANDS AND THE ISLE OF MAN

Jersey and Guernsey have slightly varying legal systems, but in either case, it is usual to qualify in another jurisdiction before taking additional examinations and training. Those qualified in the UK as a solicitor or barrister would typically take a short course in Norman Law (run by the University of Caen in France), plus local exams.

In the Isle of Man, those who have qualified and completed all the stages of their training as solicitors or barristers in England and Wales, must take two years' articles (the equivalent of a training contract) with a Manx advocate and then pass the examinations for the Manx Bar.

CHAPTER 6

A career as a barrister — what do barristers do?

Barristers (known as advocates in Scotland) are often called 'counsel'. There are around 9 000 of them in England and Wales. They are specialist legal advisers, trained to provide independent guidance to clients on the strengths and weaknesses of their legal case. However, their main work is to conduct cases in court. When a case comes to trial in a superior or a criminal court it is usually barristers who present the case and cross-examine witnesses.

Barristers cannot canvass directly for work; they are 'instructed' by solicitors with clients needing additional assistance. Normally these instructions come via the clerks who work for each barristers' chambers. On being contacted by the solicitor, the clerk will decide which member of the team would be best placed to deal with each assignment and allocate it appropriately. For the barristers concerned this may involve researching points of law and giving an opinion on the client's prospects of success or it may involve negotiation with the other side's legal team and settling issues outside of court. Of course, our main image of barristers is of them cross-examining witnesses in court. This forms a substantial part of any barrister's job, but is it as glamorous as it seems? One very experienced barristers' clerk sums it up by saying: 'It's not like Judge John Deed: it's more like Rumpole!' – a reference to John Mortimer's fictional barrister who has been defending petty miscreants for over 40 years.

Case Study 5
Matthew Jones is a junior barrister in a criminal set.

My first cases were defending people accused of run-of-the-mill motoring offences in a magistrates' court on the outskirts of London. It was a long way from the cut and thrust of courtroom drama! To be truthful, it's typical of what a lot of newly qualified criminal barristers do – petty crime such as shop-lifting, breach of the peace etc. I really thought I'd arrived when I dealt with a case of affray – that was a step up from my usual caseload! But these cases are as important as anything more high profile to those accused or involved and, for the barrister, they're a good chance to sharpen your skills. Since then I've worked in a junior capacity at Crown Court level – part of the team supporting the leading barrister, researching legal niceties, reading and hearing evidence then picking up key points to help our client and occasionally being asked to do routine cross-examinations. You learn something new every time – a lot of techniques I now use have come from observing more experienced counsel.

Crime is just one specialist area of practice in which barristers work. They normally specialise right at the beginning of their careers, choosing a pupillage in chambers which have a reputation in a particular field. This could be common law, chancery, human rights, employment, civil law, public law, employment, family law or one of several other distinct areas of legal practice. Some chambers have 'mixed sets', that is, they cover two or three specialisms, such as common law and crime.

WHERE DO THEY WORK?

Barristers may be self-employed or employed. If they are
self-employed, they must operate as a sole practitioner, usually
from offices, known as chambers, which they share with a set of
other barristers. This enables the set to share the cost of rent and
administrative services, with costs usually split on the basis of
seniority, level and amount of work.

> **LEGAL FACTS**
>
> **Under what is known as the Cab Rank Rule, if a barrister is
> available to act on someone's behalf then he or she cannot
> turn down the case.**

Barristers with three years' experience can practise independently.
This means they can work from home if they choose.

WHAT DO BARRISTERS EARN?

Most barristers would describe themselves as 'comfortable'! Top
self-employed barristers and advocates may earn a great deal of
money – many high-level cases attract six-figure fees. If you are
being paid on a high hourly rate and the case continues over weeks
and months, then your earnings are likely to be impressive. But,
however good a barrister's reputation is, he or she may not know
where their next job is coming from and for those just starting out,
pay can be low and infrequent. It takes time to build up a base of
instructing solicitors and to get your work seen and heard so that
other lawyers will remember you when they are choosing counsel
or picking a junior team to help them in court. Despite the fact
that we often envisage criminal cases when we think of what
barristers do, crime is the least well-paid specialism at the Bar.
This is mainly because, unless you are a top-flight counsel, you
could be dealing with petty misdemeanours and clients funded
by Legal Aid.

HOW DOES THE WORK DIFFER FROM THAT OF A SOLICITOR?

The key differences between self-employed barristers and solicitors are defined below.

- **No regular salary and the need to generate their own income** – although they cannot approach solicitors to give them cases, they need to keep themselves visible, so that both the potential instructing solicitor and their own clerks will remember them when the right case comes up! They should also be able to live with uncertainty – not knowing when their next job will come in or when they will be paid, since this might be months after the case concludes.

- **Less client contact** – it is normally the solicitor who deals with day-to-day matters regarding the client and keeps in touch with them by phone and mail. A barrister will see the client for a 'con' (conference) at certain points, but rarely on a regular basis.

- **More work in isolation** – this involves studying past cases and points of law, reading and forming opinions, then formulating arguments and presenting them in court or other proceedings such as employment tribunals. Barristers may bounce ideas off colleagues, but their initial research is often done alone. Only on major cases might they work as part of a team both in preparing the case and in court.

- **Advocacy** – although solicitors now have 'rights of audience' by being allowed to speak on behalf of their clients in most types of court proceeding, very few of them have chosen to exercise this beyond the magistrates' court, county court or similar level. It is still the barrister who sets out arguments on behalf of each client, responds to the opposing counsel and has to deal with new evidence and information as it arises.

LEGAL FACTS

It is possible for qualified lawyers to switch from being a barrister to working as a solicitor and vice versa. Barristers can take the Qualified Lawyers Transfer Test, solicitors do the Bar Council Aptitude Test.

For those barristers who find it difficult to break into a set or who prefer more job security, there are other options, such as the CPS, local and central government departments and in-house work, all of which are outlined in Chapter 5. The type of work that they do in these organisations does not vary from their colleagues who are qualified solicitors.

SKILLS NEEDED

In many aspects of the work, a barrister uses the same skills as a solicitor, but as a counsel there is greater emphasis on:

- negotiation and mediation (many cases never reach court, or if they do there are compromises to be made to achieve a satisfactory result)

- research, drafting and writing of coherent, original and legally sound advice, opinions and ways of approaching the case

- advocacy in terms of formulating tactics, presenting these successfully in court and adapting these as the need arises.

In a nutshell, barristers need to be able to see both the detail *and* the bigger picture, to be quick thinking and articulate and able to speak and write fluently and persuasively.

TRAINING TO BE A BARRISTER IN ENGLAND AND WALES

There are four main stages that you must complete in order to become a barrister:

● Academic stage

● Vocational stage

● Pupillage

● Tenancy (including CPD and, for those recently called to the Bar, a New Practitioners Programme).

FIGURE 2: TRAINING AS A BARRISTER IN ENGLAND AND WALES

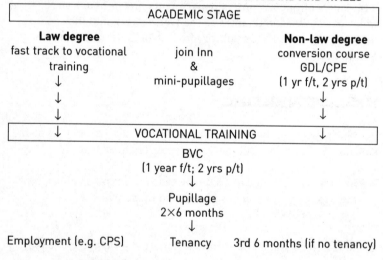

ACADEMIC STAGE		
Law degree	join Inn	**Non-law degree**
fast track to vocational training	&	conversion course GDL/CPE
↓	mini-pupillages	(1 yr f/t, 2 yrs p/t)
↓		↓
↓		↓
↓ VOCATIONAL TRAINING ↓		
	BVC	
	(1 year f/t; 2 yrs p/t)	
	↓	
	Pupillage	
	2×6 months	
	↓	
Employment (e.g. CPS)	Tenancy	3rd 6 months (if no tenancy)

ACADEMIC STAGE

Entrants need a law degree, or a non-law degree plus a GDL/CPE conversion course, details of which you can find in Chapter 5. Those without a degree but with a professional qualification may be eligible to apply through the mature students' entry route, but this is rare. Whatever route you choose, competition is very tough and even those who make the grade are not guaranteed a job at the end of the process.

While there are no specific subjects that should be studied prior to university at either GCSE or A level or the equivalent, most chambers and employers do consider the grades gained in these examinations when making their selections for pupillages.

The standard requirement for completion of the academic stage is a 2:2 Honours degree.

When considering law degree courses you need to make sure that the course you choose is a qualifying law degree that will lead directly to the vocational stage of training (see Chapter 5). A list of qualifying degrees can be found in the training section of the Bar Council website (see Useful Addresses).

VOCATIONAL STAGE: BVC

The BVC aims to make sure students intending to become barristers gain the skills and knowledge they need to cope with the specialised training and work they will undertake in their pupillage.

It's not easy to be accepted on to the BVC. The most recent figures suggest that the 1 750 places available were vastly oversubscribed and over 30 per cent of applicants were unsuccessful.

The BVC runs for one year full-time and two years' part-time. It is available at ten colleges.

● BPP Law School, Leeds

● BPP Law School, London

● Bristol Institute of Legal Practice

● Cardiff Law School

● City Law School, London (formerly known as the Inns of Court School of Law)

● College of Law, Birmingham

● College of Law, London

● Manchester Metropolitan University

● Nottingham Law School

● University of Northumbria, Newcastle.

Part-time courses are also available in some institutions.

Applications are made online at www.bvconline.co.uk. The deadline for the opening round is in early November. The second round, for those who did not apply in the autumn or those who did but were not given a place, starts in April. Full-time course fees range from around £10 000 to about £15 000, with courses in London being the most expensive.

The main skills taught on the BVC are:

● **case work skills and fact management**
case preparation
legal research

● **written skills**
general written skills
opinion writing (giving written advice)
drafting (drawing up various types of documents)

● **interpersonal skills**
conference skills (interviewing clients)
negotiation

● **advocacy**
court or tribunal appearances.

The main areas of knowledge taught are:

● criminal litigation (remedies and sentencing)

● civil litigation

● evidence

● professional ethics

- two optional subjects selected from a choice of at least six which typically includes advanced civil or criminal litigation, family practice, pro bono, judicial review practice, immigration practice and employment practice.

Assessment of skills and knowledge is done for all subjects and takes place in a number of ways, including multiple-choice tests, written papers and practical exercises which may be videoed.

Currently the Bar Standards Board is considering changes to the BVC, including a new name, a revamped syllabus and a pre-entry test. More details can be found at www.barstandardsboard.org.uk.

INNS OF COURT

Before registering for your BVC vocational training, you must become a member of one of the Inns of Court. Many students choose to do this at an early date in order to use an Inn's facilities. Once you've selected an Inn, you cannot then change, so take time to make a decision! Your choice of Inn has no effect on the area of law you want to practise or your chance of pupillage or tenancy. All Inns offer scholarships, prizes and competitions and employ student officers to help would-be barristers meet more senior lawyers who can offer advice and help with their careers. You can join an Inn well before starting your BVC – many students do this while still undergraduates or on the GDL/CPE.

There are four Inns of Court, all based in London:

- Lincoln's Inn

- Inner Temple

- Middle Temple

- Gray's Inn.

In order to be called to the Bar, you need to complete 12 qualifying units. These can be achieved in a number of different ways:

- weekends either in the Inn or at a residential centre

- education days (these are primarily for out-of-London students)

- education dinners (with lectures or talks)

- domus dinners (when students and seniors dine together)

- social dinners.

The weekend events count as three units, the days as two and the dinners as one. The Inns of Court have been around since medieval times and the practice of dining in 'your' Inn before qualifying as a barrister dates back many hundreds of years.

The Inns also organise advocacy events for students and have their own student societies which hold debating and social events. Not all events are held in London but for those that are some law schools provide transport to the appropriate venue.

LEGAL FACTS

Although the largest concentration of barristers' chambers is in London, in the Inns of Court part of the City, there are chambers in many major cities, linked to the Crown Court 'circuits' of England and Wales. In fact, the biggest set is not in London, it's in Birmingham!

PUPILLAGE

This is the final stage in becoming a barrister and it is a very tough one. Latest statistics show that there are about 1800 students on the BVC each year and less than 600 pupillages. Not everyone on the BVC applies for pupillage – a high proportion may be overseas students with jobs already fixed up at home or UK students who will opt for the CPS or other employed roles. Nonetheless, the odds can look daunting, so it's understandable that not all students will obtain a pupillage at the first attempt. (See Chapter 8 for advice on improving your chances of gaining a pupillage.)

Pupillage is like an apprenticeship – an opportunity to learn on the job while being supervised by an experienced barrister, now called a pupil supervisor (though still known by its old title of pupil master in some quarters). By this stage you will have decided on the area of law in which you wish to work, since most sets focus on only or two types of legal work, the main categories of which are described on pp. 24–25. It is paid at a minimum rate of over £800 a month plus reasonable training expenses. Many pupillage providers also guarantee earnings in the practising six months. Pupillage takes place either in barristers' chambers or, less commonly, in a legal organisation or department and is in two parts:

● months 1–6, known as the non-practising six

● months 7–12, known as the practising six.

The two sixes can take place in separate locations or different specialist areas of law. During the non-practising six you accompany your supervisor to court and read the supervisor's pleadings and other documents. You continue with this in the practising six while taking on your own cases with the permission of your supervisor.

During your pupillage, in order to be entitled to a full qualification certificate, you are required by the Bar Council to attend:

● an advocacy training course

● an advice to counsel/practice management course and

● a forensic accountancy course.

Advocacy training should be completed early in a pupillage.

The advice to counsel course aims to provide a bridge between pupillage and practice and covers:

● personal and business finance

● European Convention on Human Rights

● conditional fees

● ethics, professional conduct and complaints procedure

● professional relationships with solicitors and

● practical advice from the bench about first appearances in court.

The forensic accountancy course introduces practitioners to the use of financial and accounting information in practice at the Bar.

Further information about pupillages is available on the Bar Council website: www.legaleducation.org.uk.

TENANCY

Once the pupillage is completed, the barrister has to look for a permanent tenancy in a set of chambers. This is the final hurdle and is perhaps the hardest yet. You might be invited to join the set where you did your training but, as there are more pupillages than places in chambers, some barristers are bound to be disappointed. Some sets will invite unsuccessful pupils to do a third six which may enhance their chances if further opportunities arise or if they seek work with another chambers. However, some barristers never do manage to find a tenancy and, after all that hard work and training, have to think of alternatives, such as the employed Bar or other possibilities outlined in Chapters 12 and 13.

BARRISTERS' TRAINING IN OTHER BRITISH JURISDICTIONS

Much of the general advice and information about the work of a barrister given earlier in the chapter also applies to work in Scotland, Northern Ireland and offshore jurisdictions, so don't neglect to read it and apply it to your particular situation!

TRAINING FOR ADVOCATES IN SCOTLAND

The profession is small – currently fewer than 600 self-employed advocates are practising in Scotland, many of them as QCs. Most advocates' chambers are based at the Advocates Library in Parliament House, Edinburgh.

Trainee advocates are called intrants and they take the same full-time Diploma in Legal Practice course as trainee Scottish solicitors (detailed in Chapter 5). Following this they train for 21 months in a solicitor's office for which they receive a salary as laid down by the Law Society of Scotland. The final stage of the process is approximately nine months of unpaid pupillage known as 'devilling', spent with a member of the Scottish Bar. Devils help their devil master with the preparation of cases and accompany him or her to court and will usually spend time with another advocate so they see a variety of work. They also do some work on behalf of the Free Representation Unit. During this whole period they participate in short practical skills courses covering areas similar to those described on the BVC. Written and verbal advocacy is tested towards the end of the Intrant's training.

Applications for devilling should be made by late October of the year before you wish to commence this stage, but the Faculty of Advocates can advise further on when to apply to which devil masters.

> ### LEGAL FACTS
>
> **'Devilling' also exists at the Bar of England and Wales, though its meaning is slightly different there, relating to the sub-contracting of work by a qualified barrister who has too much on his or her plate.**

TRAINING FOR BARRISTERS IN NORTHERN IRELAND

As in Scotland, there are fewer than 600 barristers in Northern Ireland, nearly 80 of them QCs. Students wishing to become barristers in Northern Ireland must have an approved law degree. They will spend a short period shadowing a practising barrister and working in a Citizens Advice Bureau (CAB), before taking the one-year full-time degree of Barrister at Law at the Institute of Professional Legal Studies, Queen's University Belfast. This is highly competitive with at least 10 times more applicants than places. This is followed by 12 months' pupillage under a barrister before a pupil receives a Practising Certificate and is therefore fully qualified.

TRAINING IN THE CHANNEL ISLANDS AND ISLE OF MAN

For those wanting to work in offshore jurisdictions, it is usual to qualify in one of the four UK countries or possibly in Europe. See Chapter 5 for more detail on this.

CHAPTER 7

Training contracts – how to find one

So, after working hard at your A levels/Highers, gaining a degree and completing your LPC (or Diploma in Scotland and Ireland), you reach the last challenge – finding a training contract. Competition is intense and without one you cannot qualify as a solicitor.

The training system is becoming much less rigid. In England and Wales, it is now possible to do a part-time training contract – often while studying – and also to gain exemption from part of the contract if you have substantial relevant experience, for instance as a paralegal. This needs to be sorted out with your employer and with the appropriate authorities, such as the Law Society and the Solicitors Regulation Authority.

ALWAYS LOOK ON THE BRIGHT SIDE

Firms can afford to be fussy. Some top legal names calculate that they have 1000 applicants for 100 training contracts. The biggest and most prestigious firms expect a 2:1 or 1st Honours degree. They also want 340 (or more!) UCAS points.

The same firms are also more likely to market to legal departments in the older, more traditional universities, which demand the highest entry requirements, rather than the newer universities. However, as a spokesperson from a legal firm pointed out: 'that doesn't mean we're not interested in individual students from all universities.' In other words, it's up to you to be proactive and research who wants what, when they receive applications and what opportunities they offer in terms of placements prior to application.

As a trainee solicitor you will receive a salary during the period of your training contract and current rates have been detailed in Chapter 5.

However, it costs a firm around £150 000 to train you so it is in their interests to find the right people for their training and many of them put a great deal of time and energy into this procedure. They will want the brightest and the best – and even some of those students who come into this category do fall by the wayside when it comes to applying.

THINK POSITIVE

What is needed is calm, careful planning. Try to keep a sense of proportion even if things are not going the way you want.

Aim for balance in your life. Don't spend all your time with friends who are either in the same situation as yourself, or, on the other hand, with those who have training contracts and who make you feel like a failure in comparison.

TO BE FOREWARNED IS TO BE FOREARMED

At the beginning of this book you were advised to plan ahead and to think carefully about exactly what sort of legal career you wanted before applying for undergraduate courses.

If you are aiming for the top law companies, decisions need to be made well in advance in the world of legal training. Their recruitment is done about two years in advance. Undergraduates taking a law degree should be applying for training contracts at the end of their second year, while those studying for a non-legal degree should be doing so by the end of their final undergraduate year.

Smaller firms have a shorter lead time; if you are aiming at the high street or local authorities, for instance, training contracts may be advertised only months or weeks in advance. Familiarise yourself with the recruitment schedule adopted by the sort of practices that you are targeting so that you meet deadlines and can focus on your studies at the right times.

The type of questions you need to sort out at an early date include the following.

● What do you really want from your career?

● What sort of working environment do you want?

● In which sector of the law would you like to specialise?

● In which area of the country do you want to live and work?

Don't skip past these questions because you're prepared to go anywhere and do anything. That way you're not being realistic – you're merely avoiding important issues. Your future employers will expect you to have thought through these issues and you will be asked to explain your choices on application forms and be quizzed further at interview.

Is your heart set on working for a large multinational organisation in a city, or would you prefer a smaller firm where you know everybody and everyone knows you?

While you can't afford to be too exclusive, you need to consider carefully where you want to live for what may be the rest of your working life. Is it important to stay within reasonable travelling distance of your family? If it is, perhaps you should limit your search for a training contract to a particular region of the country. Are you, on the other hand, addicted to urban buzz? If so then you could look

at firms in four or five major cities. ('City' law firms do operate
outside London!)

Once you've decided on your geographical area the next step is to
research firms in that location and consider carefully those that
seem to offer what you're looking for.

BE SURE THAT YOU ARE CLEAR ABOUT WHAT A TRAINING CONTRACT INVOLVES

As a trainee, you are there to learn for two years, but also to make
a contribution to the firm. You will be dealing with real problems,
documents, cases and clients. You will typically do four 'seats' (work
in four different specialist areas), though some firms offer as many
as six and in the bigger firms you might choose to do one of these
with a business client or with a legal firm abroad. For each seat
you will be supervised and expected to keep a record of what you
have done. You will accompany more experienced solicitors to
meetings and court proceedings and help them with research and
administration. Sometimes you may be asked to do routine tasks –
these are a necessary evil! Take every opportunity to volunteer for
interesting work, to go the extra mile, to learn from others and to
work towards your career goal, such as specialising in a particular
topic.

WORK PLACEMENTS

These play a vital role in gaining a training contract and can almost
act as a trial period. Many trainees are offered training contracts by
firms where they had work placements. For further information, see
Chapter 9.

DETECTIVE WORK

The Law Society recommends the following methods for finding out
about legal firms with a view to applying for a training contract.

- Visit law fairs at your university or college and talk to as many people as possible.

- Get on to firms' websites and find out what they have to say about themselves.

- The following websites are gold mines of information:
  www.prospects.ac.uk
  www.lawcareers.net
  Legal Times www.legalease.co.uk
  Law Society Gazette www.lawsociety.org.uk
  Law Society website www.juniorlawyers.lawsociety.org.uk.

- So are the directories listed below:
  The Legal 500 by John Pritchard, published by Legalease
  Chambers & Partners Directory, published by Chambers & Partners Publishing
  Solicitors' Regional Directories, published by the Law Society.

Your university careers department will have free directories such as the *Training Contract and Pupillage Handbook*, so these will also form the basis of your research.

Also useful are:

- *The Lawyer* magazine

- *Lex* magazine – aimed at students and distributed to universities and law colleges

- *Legal Action Bulletin* – available from the Legal Action Group, 242 Pentonville Road, London N9 UW.

LIFE DOESN'T END WITH THE BIG FIRMS

There are currently nearly 10 000 law firms in private practice, of which the vast majority have fewer than 10 partners, so confining training contract applications to large firms is not a good idea.

Other possible providers of a training contract are:

● the CPS (see Useful Addresses)

● the Government Legal Service (see Useful Addresses)

● industry and commerce – in-house departments occasionally take on trainees

● the public sector – particularly local authorities such as borough and county councils.

HOW MUCH IS ENOUGH?

It is common sense to find out as much as possible about a firm before applying for a training contract, but how much should you know?

You need to demonstrate that you genuinely want to work in a particular firm through an awareness of the type of client it attracts and its recent activities, which can be found on a firm's website. You should also find out who its immediate competitors are and what they are doing and what is happening in areas of law in which the practice specialises.

Firms are looking for a sense of commercial awareness because, after all, they exist to make a profit, so an understanding of the world of business gleaned from the business sections of broadsheet national newspapers and legal magazines is expected. They will also expect you to have a grasp of current affairs – for instance, how the current economic situation might impact on legal and business situations locally and nationally.

QUALITY NOT QUANTITY

Your application form needs to reflect the knowledge you have. Firms are looking for someone who will fit in with the ethos of their organisation, who really wants to work for them and who will bring in a return for their investment.

HINTS AND TIPS FOR MAKING APPLICATIONS THAT WORK

- Firms are not impressed by an application form that shows no **specific knowledge** of their work, does not match your **skills** to their **job description** and that has clearly been sent off with 50 or so others in the mistaken belief that by trawling the net as widely as possible you're bound to catch something. Recruiters can easily spot a standard letter or CV or a statement that has been cut and pasted from another application form.

- Make sure you spend **sufficient time** on each application and show those who will be reading it that not only are you right for them, but that you believe they are right for you. On a practical note, **keep a copy** of every application form you send off, then if you are called for an interview you can check what you wrote beforehand.

- Most application forms are now **online**. It's best to copy these into a Word document and do the first and final **drafts** in this format, saving as you go along. That way you have a copy and you can proofread and double check it before sending.

- On application forms – **answer the question**! If you can't follow this sort of basic request, it doesn't bode well for your future as a lawyer. Irrelevant answers mean that your application will not make it through the first sift. Ask yourself which skills and evidence they are looking for and make sure that your answers address these.

- **CVs** should be two pages in length and be **tailored** to individual firms' requirements. They should include as much relevant **legal experience** and background as possible, even at the expense of other activities, such as casual work. Highlight any work or placements in legal firms, departments or organisations; it doesn't matter if it was unpaid – it is still relevant! Go into detail about your relevant academic work, membership of university law societies or pro bono activities done at college.

Beyond this, what do legal recruiters look for?

One HR officer in a major law firm flagged up the following.

- **Meeting the minimum requirements** – if a 2:1 is requested, don't think your 2:2 will go unnoticed. As most applications are computerised, it will probably be weeded out immediately.

- **Fluent written English** – no clichés, no parroting back of what is on our website, but something more original and in depth.

- **Relevant answers** – often candidates don't give appropriate or strong examples of the skills that we are seeking.

- **Concise answers** – often there is a word count. Not only do we not have the time to read lengthy responses, being succinct is vital for any lawyer.

- **Good spelling, grammar, punctuation** – after all, if you can't run a spelling or grammar check, then you don't have the attention to detail that's needed! If your CV is accompanied by a cover letter, this should also be word perfect not to mention businesslike and professional.

- **A hint of personality!** – we get hundreds of applications, try and stand out from the crowd rather than trotting out what you think we want to hear!

THE ASSESSMENT DAY

The next hurdle could well be the assessment day. A growing number of legal firms are opting for this method of selection, so be prepared.

Together with a group of other potential trainees you'll spend a day with a firm taking part in different activities. No two firms' assessment days are the same, but be ready for any of the following.

- **Communication and role-play exercises** where, for example, you may be asked to interview a new client or discuss a legal or current affairs issue in a group.

- **A formal interview** with a partner based on your application form.

- **Psychometric testing** – these are usually short multiple-choice, written tests. Their aim is not to test what you know, but to give an indication of the type of person you are.

- **A written exercise** such as a case study or drafting of a business letter.

- **Lunch** with the assessment group and members of the firm. Yes, this is still part of the assessment process! They are looking to see how you will interact with future colleagues and clients, so don't let your guard slip.

Firms are not interested in the level of your legal knowledge on assessment days. They want to learn about you as a person. The possibility for advance preparation may be limited, but bear in mind that your formal interview will be based on what you wrote on your application form, so a spot of revision is essential. You can anticipate certain likely questions – such as why you chose the firm, what makes you interested in law, why you want to be a solicitor, what you have gained from your studies or your work experience and what your strengths and weaknesses are – so have some answers prepared.

HONESTY IS THE BEST POLICY
Don't pretend to be someone you're not in order to try and impress people. You could be with one firm for the rest of your working life and that's a long time to keep up a pretence. Be yourself, but the best of yourself.

CREATING THE RIGHT IMAGE
Present yourself well and professionally. A dark dress or a suit with a plain light-coloured shirt is the safest bet. It's fine for women to wear formal trousers if they prefer that to a skirt. Choose clothes that are neat and professional, but also comfortable. Shoes that cripple you, a shirt that strangles you, or a hairstyle that refuses to stay in place are not going to help you on the day. Tie long hair back – you want to look like a lawyer not a student. Keep jewellery simple and hide any piercings or tattoos.

Show a genuine interest in the people you meet and try not to see everyone else as competition. Lunch is usually a good chance to ask informal questions and to find out what a firm is really like. Relax and enjoy it, but steer clear of alcohol if it's on offer and keep a clear head for the afternoon.

Don't feel you have to ask questions in order to stand out from the rest. There may be points you want to make but then again there may not, and asking something just for the sake of letting your voice be heard can be counter-productive. Have some questions up your sleeve, but don't raise anything that you could (and should) have learned from the website. Ask instead about key developments in the firm or the way that recent business or social trends have affected it.

PRACTICE MAKES PERFECT

University careers services often run assessment day workshops, mock interviews and, if you are at university or law school, your careers service should be able to give you a practice interview and also a try at doing psychometric tests: the most useful for intending lawyers are the Watson Glaser or the GAP series.

These events are well worth attending and an excellent way of preparing yourself for what could lie ahead. If you do not have access to these, try www.prospects.ac.uk or buy a couple of books that will give you hints and mock questions for interviews and tests.

CHAPTER 8

Finding a pupillage in England and Wales

NOTE Advocates and barristers elsewhere in the British Isles do not access training in the ways described below, but the tips on interviews, assessments and self-marketing are universally applicable!

A pupillage is the final part of barrister training. The structure of pupillages is covered in Chapter 7. While you will be qualified as a barrister on completion of your BVC, in order to practise you must complete 12 months' pupillage.

AN EARLY START

To give yourself the best possible opportunities in such a competitive environment you need to start early. Chambers look to recruit pupils a year to two years into the future.

There is a set timetable for applications, outlined below, but before you even start filling in the form, you need to undertake at least one – but ideally more – mini-pupillage.

MINI-PUPILLAGES

These are effectively unpaid periods of work shadowing or work experience in chambers, vitally important opportunities to see for yourself the truth about life in chambers and how one chamber differs from another. Usually they last around a week, but they can be as short as one day. They can begin when you're still at school and carry on throughout university. Many barristers do five or six mini-pupillages in order to gain a rounded view of the role of a barrister.

Mini-pupillages also provide a vital opportunity to make an impression on chambers and to demonstrate your potential. Chambers will be looking for legal experience as well as academic qualifications from pupils and mini-pupillages are an important way of gaining such experience. Without a mini-pupillage background, you have little credibility when seeking pupillage itself.

There is more about what they involve and how to find one in Chapter 9. It's also worth considering doing a placement in a solicitor's office just so you can be sure that you are making the right decision about going to the Bar and also to gain an insight into what solicitors do. After all, you will be obtaining work from them throughout your career as a counsel.

ONE STEP AT A TIME

By the time you apply for a pupillage you should have a strong idea of the area of law in which you wish to practise. The pattern of your future working life will be dependent on these decisions. For instance, if you opt for commercial law work you will spend a great deal of time in your chambers doing written work. Whereas if you choose to specialise in criminal law you could be in court almost every day.

Before applying for a pupillage with a chamber you need to carry out your own research into:

- the type of work undertaken by a particular chamber and the type of reputation they have for this work

- how well-organised a pupillage is at a particular chamber

- the levels of work available for junior tenants (this is because your chances of being offered a tenancy at the end of your pupillage are dependent on this)

- whether you would fit in with other members of a chamber and enjoy being there for the rest of your working life.

ASKING QUESTIONS

So where do you find such information? Student handbooks are a good starting point. Websites, of course, both the general professional ones and chambers' own sites. But don't confine your search to the internet. There is no substitute for talking to people around the Inns of Court and in different sets.

The sooner that you join an Inn the sooner that you can access all sorts of opportunities to meet people in the know. Dining with other students and members of the legal profession helps you to feel comfortable socialising in a legal environment and provides a valuable opportunity for gaining some inside information. Advocacy courses run by all the Inns of Court provide excellent training plus a chance to mix with legal professionals and to find out about the current state of play. The student officers at all the Inns of Court can provide up-to-date and realistic advice about pupillage opportunities. If you haven't joined an Inn yet, make informal contacts with chambers and bear in mind that, once again, mini-pupillages are the ideal way to carry out your own on-the-spot research.

APPLYING FOR A PUPILLAGE

This is mainly done by using the On Line Pupillage Application System (OLPAS), though some chambers are not in the system and will advertise to their own schedule, not the OLPAS timetable. All pupillage providers are required to post their vacancies on the website (www.pupillage.com).

Around 150 pupillage providers are on the OLPAS system. Candidates can choose to apply to up to 12 of them in two separate sessions and all these applications are made online. The first part of the application is common to all providers and is filled in only once. The second part is specific to the individual provider and is filled in separately for each application. Once the application is released into the OLPAS system it is sent directly to the pupillage provider. The provider and the candidate then communicate by email through the (password-protected) OLPAS system.

Non-OLPAS chambers accept direct applications and candidates can apply to as few or as many of these as they wish.

Unless you find yourself unable to contemplate leaving London, applying for pupillages outside the capital can be a good idea. There are fewer of these, but they don't have so many applicants, so the odds are about even.

THE OLPAS SYSTEM

There are two application seasons, one commencing in March and closing in early May and the other opening in late August with a cut-off point of the end of September. You can apply to a maximum of a dozen OLPAS chambers in each season. Offers for the summer season are made by the end of July and for the autumn round towards the end of October.

Pupillage offers remain open for 14 days, so if you are lucky enough to be chosen, you have time to make an informed decision.

The application itself is in two parts – the first covering personal information and relevant education and experience. The second part should be tailored to the individual chambers to which you are applying. Be very careful to target this part of the application properly, by making links between what you have done and what interests you in the chambers involved. The same goes for non-OLPAS chambers. Tempting though it may be to go for them all, one customised form might be worth 10 more general applications!

SELLING YOURSELF

The advice on gaining a training contract in Chapter 7 is also relevant to finding a pupillage. Particularly bear in mind the tips on completing application forms. If you fail to produce a concise, well-worded and precisely targeted application, be it OLPAS or non-OLPAS, you will not get through to the interview round.

Chambers are looking for confident, articulate, well-rounded team players, not just legal beagles, so don't neglect other aspects of your life. Anything which has involved making presentations or public appearances (for example, college drama activities, mooting), writing (for university publications or legal journals), or using your initiative (organising events, travelling, volunteering) will enhance your prospects of reaching an interview.

PUPILLAGE INTERVIEWS AND ASSESSMENTS

Again, take heed of Chapter 7 because assessment days and interviews for intending barristers can take similar formats as those for solicitors. If anything, they are even more intensive and probing. Expect to be grilled to within an inch of your life (these people are experienced at cross-examination!), anticipate both written tests and presentations – both skills are necessary in your working life at the Bar – and expect to demonstrate that you are confident, articulate, can think on your feet and can argue logically and coherently.

Case Study 6
Clare Lewis is a pupil barrister.

The assessment day and the interview which was a part of it was an exhilarating experience to say the least! It was on a Saturday, lasted for about six hours and I was exhausted by the end of it. In an odd way, I quite enjoyed the questions because they gave me the chance to prove that I could frame a good argument and that I couldn't be intimated. Some of the interviewers went out of their way to challenge me or to catch me out. It helps if you realise that they are doing this to see how well you are standing up to pressure, rather than being nasty! The written exercises were fine. I think my spelling may have been a bit wobbly but what they were looking for was attention to detail and clear logic.

A TENANCY

Becoming a tenant in a chamber means that after years of training and effort you are on the first rung of your career as a barrister.

Around nine months into a pupillage the decision is taken whether or not to offer a pupil a tenancy. It is by no means a certainty that a pupil will be offered a tenancy, and many are unsuccessful.

If it doesn't happen, you can either apply for a third session of pupillage with another chamber or apply for a tenancy somewhere else.

CHAPTER 9

Vacation placements and mini-pupillages

SUMMER FUN

You've worked hard and the summer beckons. What will it bring: a spell in the local supermarket followed by inter-railing across Europe, a trip to Thailand with a couple of mates who know of all the best beach parties, or a chance to rest the brain and develop the tan while Greek island-hopping?

Sadly, if you're really serious about a legal career your priority for the summer is more likely to be focused on Manchester rather than Majorca and Liverpool rather than Limnos.

The summer vacation brings with it a chance to gain the practical experience that will support your legal studies and lift you a step above others when applying for training contracts and pupillages.

VACATION PLACEMENTS WITH SOLICITORS' PRACTICES

These are run by larger firms of solicitors and also by major legal organisations such as the Government Legal Service and the CPS: some of these are aimed especially at minority and under-represented groups.

The good news is that most of these placements are paid (and very well-paid too!). The less welcome tidings are that, in some cases, finding a vacation placement is as difficult, if not more so, than finding a training contract, so you'll need to put some time and effort into the procedure. Many solicitors use the vacation placement as a dummy run, almost a pre-selection process for offering a training contract, so the application cycle can be tough and rigorous. Look at the hints given in Chapter 7 about seeking training contracts, because all of it is equally relevant here. Large firms may run assessment days at which they select students for vacation placements. Advice on dealing with these is also given in Chapter 7.

WHERE TO FIND VACATION PLACEMENTS

As a first step, look at yourself. What are your ultimate ambitions? Think about your strengths, the skills and experience that are going to help you to achieve those aims. What are your weaknesses and how can you overcome them? Where do you lack experience and how can you gain it?

Then start considering the firms and organisations that are likely to offer what you're looking for. A good first point of contact is law fairs, where you can visit stands, have a chat and find out what is available. Top English law firms seeking trainee solicitors will approach leading universities across the UK, including those in Wales, Scotland and Northern Ireland.

These are often advertised with university and law school careers services and tutors, as well as on the websites of the major law firms and in free handbooks and directories aimed at law students. Pay attention to deadlines as you might have to apply for a summer placement by the end of January or February.

Some legal firms also run placements at Christmas or Easter. Beat the rush by going for these times of year, rather than July and August, but remember that deadlines are likely to be even earlier than for the summer.

Given the number of applicants, it's quite an achievement to be invited to a selection day. Those whose applications didn't quite make it may be invited instead to an open day when they can speak to solicitors and trainees and find out more about the firm.

When you are applying for training contracts you can include any attendance at vacation assessment centres and open days as part of your legal experience.

HOW LONG DO THEY LAST?

Placements usually last about three weeks. They often contain a number of scheduled social and educational activities as well as day-to-day work experience. For instance, you will be invited to drinks parties, sporting events and presentations by senior staff. On the work front, you will attend meetings and may be asked to help with cases by undertaking research or preparing documentation. At the end you will normally be given feedback on your time there and asked to comment on how you found the placement.

IF AT FIRST YOU DON'T SUCCEED

The summer vacation is approaching fast and you haven't got a placement. What do you do? Your friends will soon be off to the sun, do you give up and join them? No, there are still plenty of opportunities to gain that much-needed practical experience during the vacation.

You've not had any success with your applications to large firms running vacation schemes. Then another possibility is to turn your attention to smaller firms, to be found on almost every high street.

There are also voluntary organisations, government agencies, local councils, CABs and the in-house legal departments of commercial and industrial organisations.

None of the above may openly advertise placements but they will often respond well to a direct approach. You might be able to get a paid holiday job there or, if this isn't possible, an unpaid placement.

When you're tempted to give up, just remind yourself of the importance of practical experience to your future career and steel yourself to write another letter or to make one more phone call.

MINI-PUPILLAGES

Mini-pupillages in barristers chambers usually last around a week, and can be done at virtually every time of year. They are certainly not confined to the summer. The aim is to give students a view of what life is like doing a particular job within an organisation. Your time there could involve doing a variety of things. On a mini-pupillage you might spend most of your time with a single barrister or have a chance to visit different areas of chambers. You'll probably go to court, sit in on cons with solicitors and clients and, perhaps, do some research in the library. Don't neglect the opportunity to talk to everyone you meet and to make contacts who may stand you in good stead later. For all kinds of reasons, some 'minis', have a tendency to be less organised than placements in solicitors' firms. In this situation, use your initiative, ask to be included and volunteer to take on tasks and activities.

HOW TO FIND MINI-PUPILLAGES

These are not usually advertised, though student handbooks often indicate which sets are open to being approached for mini-pupillages. In practice, most chambers accept students on these kinds of placements as long as they can work out a mutually convenient date. If a week simply isn't possible, go for a couple of days or even just a day – a mini-mini-pupillage! The quickest method of getting in touch with chambers (if you don't have a personal contact) is to approach the practice manager or senior clerk. You could also ask the student officer of your Inn for help with some leads.

MARSHALLING

This involves a week or so shadowing a judge and perhaps helping with basic administrative duties too. It's a wonderful opportunity to see behind the scenes and discuss proceedings with senior legal staff. You might be able to arrange this through personal contacts or via your Inn. The student officer is probably the best person to approach about this in the first instance.

WHAT'S IN IT FOR ME?

The answer is a very great deal, especially if you play your cards right. Vacation placements and mini-pupillages are a chance to learn a lot and nothing is as valuable as first-hand experience. Some organisations also run 'buddy' schemes where students on placements are paired with young members of staff who look after them and chat to them informally.

The plain truth is that, unless you have a history of other experience in the legal arena such as a paid clerical role, without these sorts of placements your application for a training contract or pupillage may be disregarded. However good your academic record, recruiters may think that you have no concrete basis for your decision to work in law and no evidence of applying the practical skills which it involves.

HOW CAN I MAKE A GOOD IMPRESSION?

This is perhaps the wrong approach. Rather than wondering what people are thinking of you, concentrate on what you can gain from them.

- **Be observant** – notice what is going on, how people handle different situations, how they allocate their time.

- **Be enthusiastic** about your placement and don't keep telling people how your friends are all lying on a Spanish beach and you wish you were there, even if the rain hasn't stopped for days!

- **Ask questions** – but make sure you do so at the right time. You have an enquiring mind and there's a lot to learn, but don't leap on people like an overenthusiastic puppy the moment they've put the phone down after a 30-minute conversation with a client.

- **Be professional and discreet** – don't be tempted to enter into office politics or to repeat comments or information you hear.

- **Be punctual** and **dress** in a way that is comfortable and appropriate.

- **Be willing** to do whatever you're asked – even if popping out to buy two ham rolls and a packet of crisps doesn't quite fit in with your legal ambitions.

CHAPTER 10

Making a difference — giving added value to your applications

You're now well aware of the difficulties in gaining a pupillage or a training contract and a job afterwards. You've taken on board the advice about long-term planning and on making the best of yourself on application forms, assessment days and interviews. Is there anything else you can do to show how serious you are in pursuing a legal career, whatever the difficulties?

COMBINING THEORY AND PRACTICE

The work of both solicitors and barristers demands a combination of theoretical and practical skills. In both cases a high level of academic knowledge is required, but at the same time you need to:

● think quickly

● express yourself clearly and put over complicated matters in a way that can be understood by people who have no legal training

- get on well with people from different backgrounds

- be self-motivated with good organisational skills

- enjoy working as part of a team.

Proving you possess these skills is more difficult than demonstrating academic ability, yet these are just as necessary for success in a legal career.

WHAT ELSE CAN I DO?

There are a growing number of ways in which you can gain valuable practical skills, make useful contacts and have the satisfaction of knowing that you are doing some good. First things first, if you are still at university, join the Law Society there. You don't necessarily have to be studying law to become a member. Omitting to do this will leave an uncomfortable gap in your CV and applications. Conversely, by getting (and staying) involved with this type of activity, you will have access to talks, presentations, debates and visits that would otherwise pass you by – and all of which deserve an honourable mention at the application stage.

Once you have embarked on a postgraduate legal education there will be other opportunities to attend forums, seminars and lectures by outside speakers and law firms. Seize all of these and make time to fit them into your busy schedule. They show that you are looking beyond your regular classes and assignments and trying to add an extra dimension to your legal knowledge.

In addition, consider the following ideas.

PRO BONO WORK

Pro bono work is the provision of free or subsidised legal advice for people who would not otherwise have access to it.

Today, legal aid or public funding is only available to a very small group of people. Even those who earn the minimum wage are unlikely to be eligible. This leaves a great number of people for whom legal advice at £100 an hour is completely out of reach. Pro bono work aims to do something towards bridging this gap.

US ORIGINS
Pro bono work began in the US where there has never been a publicly funded legal system and where there has long been a tradition of lawyers and law-school students undertaking such work.

In contrast, the legal aid system established in the UK in 1948 did, until relatively recently, provide legal aid for the majority of people who couldn't afford private fees.

SOLICITORS PRO BONO GROUP
The Solicitors Pro Bono Group (SPBG) was established in 1996 by Lord Phillips of Sudbury and a group of solicitors who realised that many solicitors across the country were already undertaking pro bono work and that, in order to benefit the people most in need, a co-ordinated approach was needed.

Today, the SPBG is a charity with a complete mix of members, including students, solicitors, voluntary bodies, organisations and corporations. Members don't undertake to carry out a set amount of pro bono work. However, they are required to ensure that any work they undertake is of a high standard.

The SPBG is concerned that pro bono work is never seen as a second-rate service. Student members are properly supervised and insured.

Core costs and the running of the group are almost entirely funded by membership fees. Students pay a small annual charge a year for information and support on pro bono projects.

STUDENT GROUP
The SPBG has been involved in setting up practical clinics at universities and law schools where students have an opportunity to give legal advice. Most institutions offering postgraduate legal education will provide the chance to help with pro bono activities, although the law of supply and demand means that some students

will be unlucky and not get any work while others may only have the chance to assist with just one case. The group aims to establish its network across the UK from London to other major cities and into rural areas.

THE BAR PRO BONO UNIT
Also set up in 1996, the Bar Pro Bono Unit now has over 2000 barrister members, including 80 QCs. Each member promises to give three days' unpaid work a year, which means that as much as 50 000 hours of free legal work are potentially available each year.

One of the unit's aims is to ensure that the barrister undertaking a pro bono case is as experienced as a paid barrister undertaking similar work.

The Bar Pro Bono Unit works closely with the SPBG and a large number of referrals to the unit come from the SPBG.

In order to work as a barrister with the Bar Pro Bono Unit you need to have reached the second six of your pupillage. However, there are opportunities to work on other projects.

BAR IN THE COMMUNITY
This is open to BVC students as well as pupils and barristers. The aim of Bar in the Community is to link members to charitable organisations that would benefit from having somebody with legal expertise on their management committees.

FREE REPRESENTATION UNIT
Volunteer advocates are made up of BVC and LPC students. They undertake work for the Free Representation Unit for clients with limited means who are not eligible for legal aid. They appear before Employment Appeals Tribunals, Social Security Commissioners and the Criminal Injuries Compensation Appeal Panel. You will find out more when you are enrolled on the LPC or BVC.

Again, this sort of experience is heavily oversubscribed, so do apply as soon as you start your postgraduate course. Volunteers have access to the Free Representation Unit library and office facilities and are supported by specialist caseworkers.

IN-HOUSE ADVICE CENTRES

A number of law schools run what are effectively becoming in-house legal advice centres. These offer students an opportunity to give advice to clients on legal matters. Their work is closely supervised by a barrister or a lawyer and the cases are carefully selected for their suitability for student involvement. Student work is limited to advising clients, not representing them.

STREET LAW

This began at Georgetown University, Washington DC, and is now established in over 50 US law schools, with programmes in India, South Africa, Eastern Europe and Mongolia. The first UK Street Law scheme was piloted in 1993 at the University of Derby.

Today, most law schools in the UK run Street Law projects of various kinds. These take the form of teams of students going out into the community to talk to groups about the law as it relates to them. Groups can be based in schools, colleges, community centres, housing estates and prisons. They can be made up of asylum seekers, tenants, young people or school pupils. The sessions for young people fit into the study of citizenship which became a National Curriculum subject in 2002.

A Street Law team finds out from a group the issues that concern it. Having identified these group members go away and carry out their research, returning to give a presentation to the group and answer questions, which may involve further research. This way the group receives an overview of a particular area of law and individuals in the team have a chance to develop research and presentation skills.

A typical example of such work could be a group of residents eager to make improvements to the area in which they live. The Street Law team would research housing law and explain to the group how these laws affect them and their proposed activities.

Members of any group who need to take matters further are referred to other sources of help. All the work undertaken by the students is overseen by qualified barristers and solicitors.

THE BENEFITS OF PRO BONO WORK

Well over 50 per cent of law students are involved in pro bono work of one type or another, so make sure that you don't miss out on this type of experience.

You can't undertake such work if you are motivated only by ideas of self-advancement. You need enthusiasm for the projects in which you are involved. You have to be prepared to give up valuable time for the work and to do this well you need to have a genuine desire to make a difference.

Having said that, pro bono work brings with it a chance to hone your skills and to make contact with people who could well affect your career in a positive way.

FURTHER INFORMATION
The Students' Initiative of the SPBG keeps a database of people interested in volunteering and the opportunities available. Visit its website: www.students.probonogroup.org.uk/volunteering.

Other websites with information on pro bono work include:

- Bar Pro Bono Unit – www.barprobono.org.uk

- SPBG – www.probonogroup.org.uk

- College of Law – www.college-of-law.co.uk.

The websites of UK law schools should have this information, too.

'Anyone applying for pupillage . . . should be a first rate lawyer . . . Working with FRU (Free Representation Unit) or other voluntary work of a similar nature and mooting or public speaking would also be helpful.'

Broadway House Chambers

MOOTING

WHAT IS IT?
Mooting is the oral presentation of a legal issue or problem and is possibly the nearest a student can get to appearing in court while still at university. In some law schools mooting is compulsory, while at others it is completely voluntary. In either case mooting is a useful

supplement to a law degree and can also be enjoyed by non-lawyers as the amount of legal knowledge required is not enormous.

HOW DOES IT WORK?
In a moot two pairs of advocates argue a fictitious legal appeal case in front of a judge, who is usually a lecturer or postgraduate student. To be successful you don't necessarily have to win the legal case, but you have to make the best presentation of your legal arguments.

Moots are held internally by law schools and universities. There are also a number of moots held nationally every year.

PREPARATION
Mooters have to prepare their arguments thoroughly in advance. During the moot itself the aim is to provide a courtroom atmosphere, with mooters maintaining a suitable courtroom manner and addressing each other as they would in court.

WHAT WILL I GAIN FROM MOOTING?
It is a useful way of developing the legal skills of analysis and interpretation and the personal skills of argument and public speaking. Mooting can be hard work but it's also great fun and an ideal way to socialise while building up essential attributes. If you or your team does well in regional or national competitions with other colleges, so much the better. This is a real feather in your cap and can be highlighted on any CV or application.

Student law societies usually run their own mooting programme. Details of national and international mooting competitions can be found on www.mootingnet.org.uk.

ANYTHING ELSE?

Both pro bono work and mooting are important ways of showing how seriously you take your career aims and, as such, are well regarded by chambers and legal firms. So are initiatives like volunteering at CABs and Law Centres. Sometimes here you will just be doing routine administrative work, but that can be valuable too, as we shall see in a minute. But, in some CABs and law centres, you will be given training (such as interview skills or an update on particular legislation) that you might not otherwise obtain. Taking part in witness support schemes (where you give help and assistance to those who have to give evidence in criminal proceedings) is another possibility to consider.

So far there's been no mention of actual gainful employment in a legal environment. Given that most students have to work their way through college, if you can find any sort of position in a legal setting, it will kill two birds with one stone: earning you a living and adding to your employability as a professional.

PAID WORK IN LAW

The most hotly sought after positions are those as paralegals, a widely used term, covering different duties in different workplaces, but roughly translating into a legal assistant who does research and higher level administrative duties. Few organisations which employ paralegals will take on students without a law degree or a GDL/CPE; this is because it is necessary to have a thorough understanding of legal terms and processes. Paralegal positions are advertised on university and law school careers websites and via legal recruitment sites, but writing speculatively to law firms or the legal department of a local authority/large company is a good way of finding a job in this area.

Paralegal vacancies are often snapped up, so if you can't get your foot in the door this way, think of other administrative work that you could do. It doesn't have to be high level. Acting as a clerk or receptionist in a police station, courts service, solicitors' firm, barristers' chambers or a legal body such as the Legal Services Commission will give you a good understanding of how the law operates and could lead on to promotion posts, as well as being worth its weight in gold on your CV and applications. Which brings us on to . . .

HOW DO YOU MAKE THIS EXPERIENCE WORK FOR YOU?

It's all very well undertaking the activities mentioned in this chapter, but unless you can use them in a positive way when seeking a training contract or pupillage, you will have put in a great deal of effort to no avail.

Common errors that students make when describing any form of legal experience include:

● only mentioning bare facts, instead of going into vital detail

● reeling off a list of routine duties such as filing or faxing, rather than describing what you observed about the law , the way it is applied or how lawyers work

● saying that an experience was fascinating, interesting or enjoyable without explaining why.

Here are some suggestions as to what might work instead.

● 'Spent a week marshalling for Her Honour Judge X. Observed a highly contentious slander case and had an opportunity to discuss it with Her Honour and with counsel. Was able to see and appreciate different types of cross-examination techniques and various strategies which furthered the prosecution case. I applied these in my next practical skills class and was commended.'

● 'Worked as a receptionist in Y and Co, a regional solicitors' chain, specialising in personal injury. Aside from my usual duties, I was able to see how the paralegals, legal executives and solicitors worked and the importance of attention to detail when taking evidence and making reports. I was the initial contact for often distressed or angry clients on the phone and face to face and had to be objective and focused when dealing with them.'

● 'I spent a week on placement at Z tribunal. I found it very interesting because it enabled me to see how the legal process works, who is involved – in terms of input from legal professionals, administrators and lay members – and what challenges arise when a case is being prepared and when it is heard.'

Hopefully the above examples will help you to frame CVs and applications that show what you have done, what you have observed, what you have learned and how you have applied it, rather than making bland and generic statements. The key is in the detail and the insight!

CHAPTER 11

Can I afford the cost of training to become a lawyer?

The cost of becoming a barrister, advocate or a solicitor is heavy and financial difficulties account for a great many students changing their plans and opting for a career unrelated to law.

Both the Law Society and the Bar Council recognise financial difficulties over funding as a major concern to law students, especially those who do not receive financial support from their parents.

THE COST OF UNDERGRADUATE STUDIES

The National Union of Students (NUS) calculates that the average student leaves university after three years with an undergraduate degree and debts of around £15000.

THE COST OF POSTGRADUATE STUDIES

The fees for either a BVC or an LPC are between £7000 and £15000. Then there are living expenses during the course, which, based on the NUS calculations, could bring the total cost for the year to around £20000, leaving you with debts in the region of £35000 or more.

If you take a non-law degree and opt for a conversion course before going on to BVC or LPC studies, your debts will be nearer £45000-plus.

ADDITIONAL SUPPORT FOR UNDERGRADUATE STUDIES

GENERAL ACCESS FUNDS AND HARDSHIP FUNDS

These are distributed by colleges and can take the form of cash payments or repayable loans. To be eligible you have to show that you have applied for all other sources of funding, including a student loan. The minimum payment is £100 and the maximum is £3500 a year. Most payments are in the region of £350–£1350.

Colleges set their own criteria for distributing loans and success often depends on how much of their fund allocation remains at the time of your application. The best way forward is to seek advice from your college students' union or student services department.

OPPORTUNITY BURSARIES

Since 2001 bursaries of up to £3150 for a three-year course have been available from certain institutions for full-time undergraduate degree courses. To qualify you need to be from a low-income family. The amount of the award will vary according to your circumstances.

GOVERNMENT GRANTS

Currently government fee grants may also be available to undergraduates whose own or whose family income is restricted or where the family or the individual is receiving means-tested benefits.

FINANCIAL SUPPORT FOR POSTGRADUATE LEGAL STUDY

As a postgraduate student you are not eligible for a government student loan.

DISCRETIONARY AWARDS

You may be eligible for a discretionary award from your local authority. Criteria for these awards are set by each authority and vary considerably from area to area. Where they are available they are very limited. If you are interested in applying, contact your authority for dates and put your application in as early as possible.

PROFESSIONAL STUDIES LOAN SCHEMES - HIGH STREET BANKS

Professional studies loans (also known as further education loans) for law students are available at favourable rates from some high street banks. These include:

● HSBC

● NatWest

● Lloyds TSB.

CAREER DEVELOPMENT LOANS

These are operated on behalf of the Department for Innovation, Universities and Skills (DIUS) by three banks.

● Barclays Bank

● The Co-operative Bank

● The Royal Bank of Scotland.

They are available to pay for part of the course fees on vocational courses and may include payments for living expenses where courses are full time. Terms, conditions and interest rates vary between the different banks, so shop around!

To be considered for a loan you have to provide evidence that you are a UK resident and intend to use the resulting qualification to gain employment in the UK or the European Community and to show that you are unable to fund the course from other sources.

The minimum loan is £300 and the maximum £8000. Interest on the loan is paid by the DIUS during the course and for up to two months afterwards.

Information on Career Development Loans (CDL) is available from participating banks, from branches of Jobcentre Plus and on the CDL hotline on 0800 595 505.

LAW SOCIETY BURSARIES

The Law Society offers a bursary open to all GDL/CPE and LPC students who are experiencing financial hardship. It consists of a variety of grants and loans. The fund is very limited and there are competitive elements and hardship criteria. In 2007, out of 170 applications, only seven were successful.

The Law Society also runs a Diversity Access Scheme which provides support to certain students who may be facing particular obstacles such as social or ethnic barriers.

Further information and an application form can be obtained from http://juniorlawyers.lawsociety.org.uk.

Students in Scotland and Northern Ireland will find that the Law Societies there offer similar schemes.

BAR COUNCIL SCHOLARSHIP TRUST

This provides assistance during pupillage in the form of interest-free loans up to £5000 depending on your individual circumstances.

INNS OF COURT SCHOLARSHIPS

In the year 2008, the Inns of Court together offered over £39 000 000 in a range of scholarships and other awards for all phases of training from GDL/CPE to BVC and pupillage trainees. Applications are normally restricted to one Inn and are competitive, often involving essays, written statements, interviews and other exercises to decide who can benefit from these limited funds. Early applications are recommended. Information is available from student officers at each of the Inns of Court.

If you are qualifying as an advocate in Scotland, contact the Faculty of Advocates about the scholarships that they offer or the Bar Library if you are intending to practise as a barrister in Northern Ireland.

ACCESS FUNDS

These are available for postgraduates experiencing particular difficulties in meeting living costs. (See General Access Funds and Hardship Funds under the Additional Support for Undergraduate Studies section of this chapter.)

SPONSORSHIP

A number of the larger law firms throughout the UK offer sponsorship for students taking vocational law courses. If you accept sponsorship you will usually be expected to serve your training contract with that firm. In some cases you will be expected to commit to a longer period of employment. Needless to say, the competition for this type of funding is very strong, and successful students are usually expected to have consistently excellent academic grades and to back these up by producing written and oral evidence of their talent and potential.

You should be able to find out more about sponsorship opportunities from your college careers service and in publications such as *Prospects Legal* and other student handbooks distributed to law departments and careers services. *The Lawyer* magazine regularly publishes a student special supplement with a list of sponsorship opportunities.

EDUCATIONAL CHARITIES AND TRUSTS

It isn't likely that a course lasting for more than one year could be financed entirely by trust fund help. However, educational charities and trusts can provide supplementary help to students who are without funding or who need additional help.

Charities usually pay one-off sums of up to around £300 for particular items or to make the difference between completion and non-completion of a course.

Some charities and trusts are quite precise in their requirements, restricting applications to people living in a particular area, or of a certain age, or with a parent working in a specific type of employment and living in a particular area.

As many charities and trusts work at a very local level it is worth starting with your local clergy, town hall or CAB.

Advice on alternative sources of funding can be gained from the Educational Grants Advisory Service (see Useful Addresses). Further information is to be found on the website www.scholarship-search. org.uk. Your college library or careers service may also offer access to www.funderfinder.org.uk (organisations must be licensed to use this, so it is not available via open web access).

MAKING A LITTLE GO A LONG WAY

As a student, offers of money will not be difficult to find. The generosity of companies offering you loans, overdrafts and credit cards can be overwhelming. At first it may appear that despite all the dire predictions of student poverty, you need never want for anything again.

At this point it's important to remember there is no such thing as a free lunch and the companies offering you money exist to make a profit, not to do you a favour.

Especially when you are undertaking a long course of study, such as qualifying as a barrister or a solicitor, you need to start budgeting from the word go. A wild undergraduate year can make the difference between completing your studies and dropping out.

Many college student services, or NUS welfare services, offer money management and debt counselling services and these are well worth attending early on in your studies before matters get out of hand.

REALISTIC RESEARCH
If you've lived at home before going to university and relied on pocket money or the odd holiday job for money, a cheque for several thousand pounds can seem like an unending source of finance.

A recent survey revealed that around 50 per cent of sixth-formers either underestimated or had no idea what their expenses would be at university.

The cost of living can vary enormously from area to area and if money is going to be tight, it's a good idea to look into local costs of accommodation and the availability of part-time work before you put in your application.

Also, make sure you're aware of your entitlements and take advantage of discounts available to students through using your NUS card at www.nusonline.co.uk.

KEEP A NOTE OF WHAT YOU SPEND

You wouldn't be human if you've never put your card in a cash machine and been horrified at the small amount the unforgiving screen insists you possess.

However, for your own peace of mind you need to keep close tabs on where your money is going and what debts you have.

Before using your credit card to tide you over in difficult times, or before buying from a catalogue, check the interest rates and repayment conditions. Even a small slip from the repayment terms can bring severe penalties.

WHICH BANK WANTS MY OVERDRAFT THE MOST?

The answer is that at first sight all of them are fighting to offer you terms you just can't refuse. Cash refunds and retail discounts rank among the most common incentives you'll be offered to deposit your funds in a particular bank.

Don't be carried away by the generosity of these offers – take time to look at the small print. Check the interest rates for an account in credit and for an unauthorised overdraft. See if there is a branch near to your place of study and whether the branch has a student staff officer attached.

When embarking on legal training it's well worth checking a bank's graduate account arrangements, including preferential rates on loans and interest-free overdraft opportunities.

PART-TIME WORK

Research by the NUS revealed that over 41 per cent of students questioned did part-time work during term time. Many students feel they have to take paid work in order to meet their basic living costs.

If you know you will need to take part-time work in term time to support your studies, check whether the institutions to which you are considering applying have employment agencies run by student unions or whether the careers service advertises part-time and vacation work; most do! If you can secure a job that is related to law, so much the better. See Chapter 10 for some hints on where to look.

FURTHER INFORMATION

The NUS Welfare Unit produces a series of excellent information sheets covering finance and other student-related issues (see Useful Addresses).

PUBLICATIONS

- *A Guide for Individuals in Need*, published by the Directory of Social Change (DSC) – www.dsc.org.uk

- *Directory of Grant Making Trusts*, also published by the DSC – www.dsc.org.uk

- *Charities Digest*, published by Waterlows Legal Publishing

- *The Grants Register*, published by Palgrave Macmillan Publishers Ltd – www.palgrave.com.

CHAPTER 12

Coping with the blips

Law is intellectually rigorous and only the most able people succeed. This can lead to the assumption that academically bright pupils should take a law degree because they are capable of gaining a place, regardless of whether the course and the job to which it leads are right for the individual.

However, be careful that the buzz you get is not from the challenge rather than the job itself.

Case Study 7
Emma Williams is a practising solicitor.

From school onwards everybody kept telling me how hard it was to be a solicitor and not to be disappointed if I didn't make it.

This made me determined to prove them wrong. I worked really hard through university and through my postgraduate course and put great effort into gaining a training contract.

Two years on, I'm not at all sure that being a solicitor is what I want. It's hard to put my finger on it. The people I work with

---

are great, the atmosphere in the office is quite relaxed. Still somehow I'm not sure the role I have at work is really me.

I fought so hard to achieve my goal, I possibly didn't give enough time to examining what the end result of my struggles would be.

'The best laid schemes o' mice an' men gang aft a-gley.'

Robert Burns

The words of the Scottish poet Robert Burns might have been written about legal training. Despite working hard, planning ahead and being as prudent as possible without joining the living dead, matters may not work out as you had hoped.

How do you cope with the blips that arise and interfere with your plans?

It's important to remain positive and flexible and remember that, trite as it may sound, when one door closes another one has a habit of opening.

What if, like Emma (in Case Study 7), you do qualify as a lawyer and then decide it's not for you? Paula (in case study 8) turned her legal training to her advantage.

Case Study 8
Paula Nixon did *begin her career as a solicitor and has now moved on. She now works for a central government financial department at a very senior level. She is based in the south of England.*

I was a solicitor with a City firm specialising in mergers and acquisitions and involved with all sorts of huge financial deals. I had always planned to build up some money and then move on. Eventually I was ready to leave London and was also tired of such pressurised work that left me no time for a private life. I was being paid a very good salary which enabled me to buy a nice house outside the capital and look for work which was still interesting and had a legal bias. I was offered this job which involves regulatory affairs, compliance, trying to prevent financial irregularities and liaising with offshore financial companies.

My legal training looked good on my CV, which landed me an interview. It also gave me the skills for this particular role where attention to detail and an understanding of how the financial markets work is important.

I enjoyed my time as a solicitor and it gave me an excellent grounding, but I've moved on now. My current post is rewarding and satisfying – no two days are the same.

Paula and Emma had both completed their training and secured the type of work that they had been striving for over many years. What sort of blips can occur earlier on?

The following scenarios are all fairly common – and can be overcome.

What if you have a law degree or a conversion course, but the future is less clear than it once was? It could be that:

● you don't have a place for the vocational stage of your training: either an LPC or BVC or their Scottish/Northern Irish equivalents

● you have a place on the GDL/CPE or a vocational course, but so far have not secured a training place, pupillage or their Scottish/ Northern Irish equivalents

● you've completed the vocational stage of training but haven't found a pupillage, training contract, apprenticeship or a devil master

- you've done well on your vocational training but a lack of relevant experience and/or poor degree grades are holding you back

- you've commenced a law degree, conversion course or vocational course but, for all sorts of reasons, may not be able to continue with your studies at the moment

- you've completed or will complete your law degree and you want to use your legal knowledge in your job, but you don't want to undertake further full-time training

- you change your mind part way through your vocational training

- after gaining your degree or vocational training you want a career that has nothing whatever to do with the law.

YOU HAVEN'T FOUND A PUPILLAGE OR A TRAINING CONTRACT/PLACE

WHAT ARE YOUR OPTIONS?

It is quite usual not to have secured the next stage of your training at the beginning of a vocational course or at the commencement of any type of conversion course such as the GDL. Many students go on to find the relevant employment during the next year or two of study. Obviously this brings its own pressures; it's very hard to combine intensive work at law school with making targeted applications, so you will need to be focused and well organised. Some people do defer any job hunting until they have finished their studies entirely. If you choose to do this, there may well be a time lapse before you find a suitable training niche. If you are applying to the major solicitors' practices which recruit well in advance this may be as long as two years, although you will know fairly early in this period whether you have been successful.

For some people, it is their lack of relevant experience that is the barrier, in which case there is an easy remedy – find some type of work or voluntary opportunity in a legal setting. This doesn't need to be high level – the sort of ideas suggested in Chapter 10 are still appropriate here. They provide the chance to upgrade your practical understanding and prove your motivation and suitability in the professional marketplace. See Jo's account (Case Study 10 on page 97) of her job search for proof of how this works!

Finally, your class of degree or other exam marks may be the cause of your being rejected early on in the application process. How can you mitigate this? Some ideas are offered under the next heading and in Justin Smith's story (Case Study 9 on page 96).

Having invested so much time, money and energy into getting where you are, the chances are the urge to continue is strong. Balanced against this is the fact that at this point, unless you've won the lottery, you're almost certainly running short of money.

YOU HAVEN'T BEEN OFFERED A PLACE ON A BVC, LPC OR SIMILAR COURSE

In these situations you need to think carefully about why you've been unsuccessful so you can strengthen future applications. One thing that might be lacking is commercial legal experience. Or your academic record may be counting against you. A way to compensate for both factors is suggested by Justin and Jo (Case Studies 9 and 10).

If your educational grades are consistently disappointing, you may have to accept that you should look for another route to qualification – such as ILEX (see Chapter 5), or for another type of legal job.

In both cases you could consider the following options.

PARALEGAL WORK
This involves working with a firm of solicitors supporting qualified staff in their work.

You bring to your job a great deal of legal knowledge, which makes you much more useful to the firm than somebody from a non-law background. At the same time, you gain hands-on experience of relevant work that looks good on your application forms.

As a paralegal you will be supervised and your work checked carefully by qualified staff, but you're likely to be given interesting tasks, such as assisting in background work, carrying out research, drafting documents and preparing material for trials.

Finding paralegal work with a firm might not lead directly to a training contract, and some firms make a point of never offering training contracts to these staff. Others use it as a sort of trial period and may later suggest that the paralegal commences a training contract with them. A few organisations explicitly look for someone who would like a training contract and this can begin once he or she has proved themselves as a paralegal. Paralegal is now seen as a career in its own right, so for those who decide not to pursue the solicitor/barrister/advocate route, opportunities still exist within this new and growing profession.

What this type of experience does do is give you a chance to gain valuable practical experience and, most importantly, to see whether legal work is right for you.

Case Study 9
Justin Smith received a 2:2 for his law degree. He tried to make up for this by studying for an LLM (a master's degree in law) and he did well on this course and also when he progressed to the LPC.

But after that I was well and truly stuck. Either the 2:2 or the fact that I had not really worked in the legal field on a sustained basis meant that I was never called for interview. In the end I took a paralegal job with an in-house legal department. My boss was keen for me to progress and ensured that I met and worked with lawyers from leading practices that we dealt with. I, in turn, gave it 110 per cent both in terms of delivering high-quality work and in maximising that network. Two years down the line, I was asked to apply for a training contract by several of the firms who had got to know me. I'm now a trainee with a well-known top regional firm.

Case Study 10
Jo Rourke is a solicitor with a legal firm in London,
specialising in entertainment law.

A lot of our clients are from the music industry and therefore
a lot of our work is contract based. However, we do
undertake a variety of other work, including litigation, which
means I also go to court now and again.

The firm is quite small and the atmosphere in the office is
relaxed and yes I do meet some famous faces!

I took a degree in European law with French and Spanish
and then took a break for a couple of years. During that time
I went travelling and took several jobs supposedly to save
up for my LPC year, although that didn't quite work out.

I started my LPC without a training contract, which was a
gamble, and I still didn't have one when I'd finished. After
my LPC, I took a paralegal job with a large city firm, working
on a project in Bristol. The work lasted for 10 months, at
which point I took another paralegal job with my present
firm. It was made clear at the interview that if we got on
well there was a good chance the firm would take me on
as a trainee and after a few months this proved to be the
case. It might be unusual for this to happen with the very
big organisations, but I think it's something that often
happens in smaller firms.

OTHER OPTIONS FOR SUCCESSFUL LAW GRADUATES

You have completed or will complete your law degree and are keen
to use the knowledge you've gained but don't want to embark on
further full-time study.

You're not alone!

Fewer than 50 per cent of law graduates enter full-time professional law training courses. One of the major reasons for this is lack of money. Unless you are receiving significant financial support from your family, getting through the academic and postgraduate stages of legal training is immensely difficult.

This means many individuals who would be an asset to the legal profession opt for different careers, leaving the jobs for those who are more financially secure, but no more talented. Both the Bar Council and the Law Society have expressed concern over this state of affairs.

ILEX

If you still want to train as a solicitor you could consider the ILEX graduate option. Your legal degree will exempt you from all examinations except for the legal practice examination. You will then have to do five years' work under supervision before studying part-time for your LPC, but you will get there and you will be earning money and building up your client base during that time (see Chapter 5).

YOU CAN'T CONTINUE WITH YOUR STUDIES

Some students do become tired or stressed or just want a break from an academic existence. If you feel as if you are on a treadmill, then it is possible to get off! You can, for instance, take time out between your degree and postgraduate legal education or between the GDL/CPE and the BVC/LPC. (This also holds true in the Scottish and Northern Irish systems). Some people use this time to gain more hands-on legal experience, others to earn more money in casual jobs such as hospitality or retail, and another group to go backpacking in far-away places. These are all perfectly valid ways to spend your time, especially if you can convince would-be employers of the skills that you have gained. Just one word of warning – don't take too long a break! More than two years and recruiters may wonder how you have kept your knowledge up to date. Also a lengthier gap may mean you fall foul of some of the regulations of the professional legal bodies.

What if you need to stop studying midway through the course? This would need to be discussed on an individual basis with your tutors, but usually a compromise or a solution can be worked out and you could return at an appropriate point a year or so down the line.

If finances are holding you back, consider alternatives to full-time study. Possibly because of the financial difficulties experienced by many students, there has been a rapid rise in the number of part-time vocational courses over the last few years. These are confined to England and Wales. At the moment there is no such provision in the Scottish and Northern Irish systems.

PART-TIME BVC COURSES

At present, these are run at City Law School, the BPP Law School in London and Leeds, the College of Law in London and Birmingham, Northumbria University, Manchester Metropolitan University and the Bristol Institute of Legal Studies. They usually last two years.

PART-TIME AND DISTANCE LEARNING LPC AND GDL CONVERSION COURSES

Combining part-time study with a full-time job is becoming an increasingly popular option. There are two main reasons for this. The first is that it avoids the massive debts that for most people are an inevitable part of full-time legal courses. The second is that it avoids periods of unemployment because students can remain in their existing jobs while seeking a training contract or a pupillage. Many providers now offer various modes of part-time and distance study.

Part-time courses may include:

● traditional evening classes held twice a week

● Saturday classes held weekly

● weekend classes covering a Saturday and a Sunday every month

● distance learning.

The last two options are a good choice if you work long hours or evenings but they do demand more self-discipline than the other study options.

FUNDING A PART-TIME COURSE

Most part-time students pay their own fees and it is quite common for colleges to accept payment on a monthly instalment basis. CDLs are also a possibility for part-time students (see Chapter 11).

A growing number of firms are offering sponsorship to part-time students so it's also worth making contact with potential employers to see what they may offer.

If you're studying for a BVC, contact the Inns of Court to find out what support they might be able give you.

CHOOSING A PART-TIME COURSE

Before making a decision:

● study college websites

● attend open days

● find out about the support given to part-time students and what books and other learning materials are provided on the course

● remember, it's helpful in planning your study schedule if you receive all the course materials at the beginning of your course

● look at the experience a college has in running part-time legal courses

● check whether the college has a specialist careers service and, if it does, what help it is likely to offer you

● look for online facilities that could help you work from home or from your office.

USING YOUR DEGREE OR VOCATIONAL QUALIFICATION IN LAW-RELATED JOBS

You don't have to be a barrister or a lawyer to use your legal knowledge in work that brings you job satisfaction and career opportunities. People with a law background and the proven skills that this involves are very marketable.

THE PRIVATE SECTOR

Many organisations have legal departments and employ people with a legal education. They range from major high-street retailers to insurance companies and computer operations. The pay is usually good with these companies and you may find you enjoy the pace of work and the opportunities such jobs bring.

Law firms themselves employ career paralegals, outdoor clerks, legal secretaries, licensed conveyancers, legal accountants, barristers' clerks, practice managers and law-costs draftspeople – to name but a few of the possibilities.

THE PUBLIC SECTOR

There are posts not only in the legal departments of county councils and district councils but also in other areas where there is a need for legal knowledge, such as planning, social services and education departments.

Central legal departments and quangos, such as the Legal Services Commission and the CPS, or the COPFS in Scotland, need high-level administrators and caseworkers. The Courts Service needs professionally qualified lawyers to act as, for instance, magistrates' clerks in England and Wales. Court stenographers are also in demand and trade unions, too, welcome professional staff with a legal background.

NOTARIES

This is a very small area (only about 900 practitioners), but certainly worth considering. More common in Europe than in the UK, notaries verify and certify legal documents for use abroad and can also advise on non-contentious legal issues. An even more specialised branch of the profession, called scrivener notaries, works only in the City of London. Prior to training as a notary, some background in law is necessary – ideally passing the LPC or BVC.

WHAT ELSE?

Other jobs with a legal element include:

- patent attorney – dealing with the legal aspects of bringing new ideas and designs into the public arena

- pressure groups and charities that take on staff with a legal background

- research – the skills you have gained on a law degree, such as clear thinking, analytical strengths, plus your legal knowledge could make you a strong contender for this type of work

- teaching – in recent years law has become a popular academic and vocational subject. You could look at taking a teaching qualification, or apply for a post teaching law

- law centres – there are 61 centres in the UK providing free legal advice and representation. All of them employ some paid staff

- media – specialist legal publishing firms such as Butterworths may be very interested in your skills and the niche area of legal journalism – writing for law journals, law student publications or, with experience, being a legal correspondent in the national media – may particularly appeal.

These are just some ideas – you may be able to think of others. Why not find out more about these and other options by consulting your careers service or using a graduate careers website such as www.prospects.ac.uk.

Case Study 11
Rachel Nixon is Executive Officer at the Ards Borough Council, Northern Ireland.

I support the town clerk and chief executive, carrying out research, preparing material for meetings, writing reports, studying and advising on the impact of proposed or actual legislation or other government policies on the council.

I'm not a qualified solicitor. I have a degree in European law with languages from the University of the West of England and I completed the LPC at Nottingham Law School.

My original plan was to complete my legal training in England and then return to Northern Ireland, but I found it difficult to get a training contract in England and for that, and a number of other reasons, I decided to return home to Northern Ireland.

The training system is different there. Competition is extremely tough and I tried two years running to gain a place at the Institute of Professional Legal Studies without success. Instead, I joined Sainsbury's graduate management programme. After working in various stores I became a member of the retail systems team, introducing new IT systems into stores. I was travelling a great deal between the UK and Northern Ireland, which was time-consuming and not very mentally challenging. When I saw my present job advertised it specified a background in law and seemed to offer everything I wanted – responsibility, challenge, opportunities and the chance to live at home. I don't regret not becoming a solicitor at all. I couldn't do my present job without my theoretical and practical experience.

I think it's important to realise there's far more to a legal career than being a solicitor or a barrister.

Case Study 12
Dilip Patel obtained a law degree, but his grades were disappointing and he reluctantly realised that he was unlikely to find the training contract that he wanted.

So I took some time out to think about what came next and, while I was doing so, I did a series of clerical jobs. These showed that I had a real flair for administration – I was well organised and methodical and I enjoyed working with the public. Then a receptionist job came up in a barristers' chambers and I realised that it meant that I could use my office skills in a legal setting. I applied for it and was selected ahead of many other good candidates. I love it here! I'm in the centre of legal London and I get to hear about everything that's going on in the world of law. It's well paid too – I'm earning more than my friends who are trainees with high-street and medium-sized firms. Maybe I'll move on to be a barristers' clerk or a practice manager – I'm certainly thinking along those lines now.

SUPPOSE YOU CHANGE YOUR MIND PART WAY THROUGH YOUR TRAINING?

This does happen (as Jennifer's story in Case Study 13 on page 113 illustrates). Whether you are still studying on a vocational course or you're actually undertaking a training contract or pupillage/ apprenticeship, you do still have options.

If you are on a course, do you continue and get a qualification out of it, even though you don't intend to use it? You may change your mind back again at a later date! And you are unlikely to recoup your course fees. So it may be a question of gritting your teeth and getting on with it. If you decide to drop out at this point, that's fine too (but remember you may have to write off all the money you have spent!). You can then move on to do the sort of alternative legal work described here or a job unconnected to your training. There are all sorts of graduate opportunities that you can go for.

If you decide to leave when you have actually commenced a traineeship, pupillage or similar role, then you could be liable to pay back any costs that your employer has incurred and will certainly have to refund any awards connected to that part of your training. You *are* a partly qualified lawyer – so read the small print! Again, you may decide to grin and bear and at least come out as a fully fledged solicitor, barrister or advocate before moving on. If not, you have the same alternatives as those outlined in this chapter and the one that follows.

How will any future employers view this scenario? Sympathetically on the whole. They realise that people do change their mind and as long as you can justify this and come up with positive reasons for your move to their sector, then they will value all the skills and training that you have acquired to date. But it is up to you to come up with a rational and reasonable explanation and to promote your interest and motivation in the new area to which you want to switch.

NON-LEGAL OPTIONS FOR LAW GRADUATES

What if, after your law degree or vocational studies, you want a career that has nothing whatever to do with law?

Read on. Chapter 13 is for you.

CHAPTER 13

Non-legal options for law graduates

Whatever you decide to do at the end of your law degree course, you will take with you on graduation a range of practical, soft or transferable skills, which will be valuable whatever your future career choices may be.

These include:

- communication skills – the ability to explain what you mean simply and clearly, both in speech and in writing

- presentation skills – arranging information and putting it forward in an informative, interesting way

- analytical skills – thinking through problems logically in order to reach workable solutions

- research skills – selecting information from reports, journals and books

- team skills – the ability to work as part of a group

- leadership skills – having the confidence to take the lead and take control of a situation

- information technology skills – as with the majority of degree courses, law courses rely increasingly on the use of computers and computerised information.

Such skills make you highly attractive to employers in a wide range of employment sectors.

OTHER OPTIONS

FINANCE

This could be high on your list as the most popular choice among law graduates opting for a non-legal career is finance.

Major reasons for this are career opportunities and financial rewards. Successful graduates in the financial sector can earn immensely high salaries.

Employers look for a good degree in any subject plus numerical, analytical, communication and interpersonal skills.

ACCOUNTANCY

Professionally qualified accountants are known as either certified or chartered accountants. Their role is to make sure clients of whatever size make best use of their financial resources. They prepare and audit accounts, prepare tax returns, diagnose financial problems, give advice on mergers and corporate finance.

Accounting divides into two main areas: financial and management.

Training is provided by a number of professional bodies (see Useful Addresses), the largest being the Institute of Chartered Accountants in England and Wales (ICAEW). It consists of a three-year training contract with an authorised training firm, combining work experience with academic study and examinations.

Law graduates may apply for credit (to study to become an associated chartered accountant with the ICAEW), providing they have completed the appropriate law modules as part of their studies. Law graduates (either single or Joint Honours) from the UK or the Republic of Ireland will automatically be awarded credit for both commercial and company law, providing a company law module has been completed.

BANKING

Many banks run accelerated or fast-track programmes for graduates. The Bank of England runs a training scheme open to graduates with any degree.

Professional qualifications are awarded by the Institute of Financial Services (IFS), which is the official body of the Chartered Institute of Bankers (CIB) (see Useful Addresses).

INSURANCE

Insurance work falls into three main groups: life insurance, general insurance and commercial insurance. The professional body responsible for training in the insurance industry is the Chartered Insurance Institute (CII) (see Useful Addresses).

THE STOCK EXCHANGE

Market traders buy and sell shares. Before working as a market trader on the Stock Exchange it is necessary to pass the domestic equity market oral examination run by the Stock Exchange and the Securities Institute.

Stockbrokers are paid a commission by clients for advising them on investments on the Stock Exchange. Stockbrokers must be registered with the Financial Services Authority.

THE CIVIL SERVICE

Provides work for nearly half a million people and comprises over 170 departments and agencies. The Civil Service looks for quality recruits from every walk of life and legal graduates are often particularly well suited to a career in the Civil Service.

Vacancies are advertised on the Civil Service website, in the press and in professional journals.

THE CIVIL SERVICE FAST STREAM

This is the Civil Service accelerated development programme that offers a series of intensive job placements designed to prepare you for senior management positions.

EUROPEAN FAST STREAM

This aims to increase the number of British graduates securing permanent posts in EU institutions. It offers four years' training and work experience intended to improve chances of success in EU recruitment competitions. Language qualifications are desirable, but can be developed during training.

EUROPEAN COMMISSION

The European Commission holds regular competitions for recruitment to its administrative grades and a legal background is seen as particularly useful.

ADMINISTRATION: CHARTERED SECRETARY

Private and public companies are required by law to appoint a company secretary and many large organisations have company secretarial departments.

Chartered secretaries are employed as company secretaries and administrators in business, commerce, education, charities, investment trusts, hospitals and local authorities.

Graduates are exempt from the first part of the Institute of Chartered Secretaries and Administrators (ICSA) qualifying examinations. They have to complete the bridging programme modules covering financial accounting, corporate law, strategic and operations management and management accounting, plus the professional programme modules of corporate governance, corporate secretaryship, corporate administration and corporate financial management.

Study is usually on a part-time basis while working in a relevant job. Around 70 per cent of trainees have their fees paid by their employers. After three years' relevant work, graduates can apply for associate membership and for fellowship after five years.

PERSONNEL OR HUMAN RESOURCES

This work involves recruiting the best people for the job and training and managing them to meet their full potential, thus making the organisation that employs them as efficient as possible. A knowledge of employment law is important, but is combined with many other duties. Openings are to be found in a wide range of public and private organisations, including department stores, supermarkets and factories, banks, health services, airlines, hotels, further and higher education institutes and travel companies. And, of course, law firms!

The Chartered Institute of Personnel and Development (CIPD) considers law, together with degree subjects such as psychology and business studies, to be particularly suited to personnel work.

The professional qualification is the CIPD Professional Development Scheme involving around two years' part-time study, usually while working in a personnel-type job.

INFORMATION MANAGEMENT

Information managers work in public or academic libraries, in legal firms, medical organisations, scientific establishments, finance, industry, commerce, the media and wherever people need to access information. Graduates with a law degree plus a librarian/ information management qualification are in a good position to find work in a legal firm.

The Standing Conference of National and University Libraries (SCONUL) scheme enables graduates who are looking for a career in library and information management to spend a trainee year working in related employment in order to gain supervised experience of the work. Employers undertake to provide trainees with an overall view of the library system and experience of the day-to-day operation of a library.

After completing the trainee year, students can go on to a full-time course, or apply for a job and either study part-time for a professional qualification or delay further study for a time.

The Chartered Institute of Library and Information Professionals (CILIP) is the professional body for librarians and information managers or specialists (see Useful Addresses).

INFORMATION TECHNOLOGY
Around half of the graduates recruited to work in the IT industry do not have IT degrees.

The use of psychometric tests as part of the selection process is becoming more widespread because the tests give employers an idea of a candidate's ability to pick up new skills.

A graduate apprenticeship programme is available, with three key elements:

- an Honours degree

- Key Skills certificates

- technical/optional units certificates selected to reflect the student's area of work.

See Useful Addresses for further information on information technology.

JOURNALISM
Graduates with degrees in any subject can make a career in journalism.

Seventy to eighty per cent of new entrants to journalism have taken a postgraduate course in journalism. Full-time courses recognised by the National Council for the Training of Journalists (NCTJ) or the Broadcast Journalism Training Council (BJTC) in various aspects of journalism are available at colleges in the UK and Northern Ireland. Part-time courses are also available.

There are still some opportunities for graduates to be recruited directly into jobs as journalism trainees on magazines and newspapers and as broadcast trainees by television companies.

PUBLISHING
The way into a career in publishing is often through a job as an editorial assistant with a publishing company.

There are postgraduate courses in publishing available at a number of universities and the Publishing Training Centre has a list of these (see Useful Addresses). However, the majority of graduates with degrees in all subjects get into publishing by taking whatever job they can.

SOCIAL WORK

Graduates who can show evidence of an interest in social work can apply to join a two-year Master's programme run at universities and colleges across the UK. Some bursaries are available to help with the financial cost of training and part-time courses are available so it is possible to have a job and gain a qualification at the same time (see Useful Addresses). This may be of particular interest to those who have some knowledge of criminal law, family law, legal aid work or human rights.

THE PROBATION SERVICE

Members of the probation service work in criminal courts giving advice on sentencing options, in prisons working with prisoners trying to change the attitudes that have led them to commit crimes, and in the community with offenders who have been given rehabilitation and community punishment orders. You may be especially drawn to in this type of role if you have the same sort of legal interests as those noted for social work.

A degree in law together with subjects such as sociology and psychology are particularly suited to a career in the probation service.

Previous relevant work experience, usually in the form of voluntary work, is essential. Professional training leads to the Diploma in Probation Studies (DipPS). This two-year training combines academic teaching and work-based supervised practice.

THE POLICE SERVICE

The service is looking for graduates with degrees in all subjects. Entry is by either the standard route or the High Potential Development Scheme. The latter aims to seek out the future leaders of the police service and to help them realise their potential through an individually tailored career development programme (see Useful Addresses).

Case Studies 13 & 14
Jennifer French finished her law degree with very high grades and did equally well on an LLM and the LPC. She had a training contract with a City law firm in the bag. It was then she decided that the law just wasn't for her! So what came next?

I had always imagined that the law was where I would make my career. All my family are in professional jobs such as medicine, accountancy and teaching and I suppose that influenced my thinking. It was only when my goal was in sight that I realised that it wasn't what I wanted. I enjoyed law but the thought of working in that particular culture for the next 40 years woke me up to the fact that I actually was better suited to something more creative. So I got a graduate trainee job with one of the major advertising agencies. Yes, I guess it sounds like worlds away from what I'd been studying, but it did actually use the sort of strengths that I'd built up over the years. It demands the confidence to generate ideas, fluent writing ability, the talent to analyse facts and situations and look for solutions, a sound business brain, plus negotiation skills. So there are parallels. But it also had that extra dimension of creativity.

Two years down the line and I've never been happier. I'm not sure I would have fitted into most law firms anyway, the less formal atmosphere here is far better.

Clare Brook had a different experience.
My A level grades were so-so, but I pulled all the stops out to get a good degree from one of the less prestigious universities and then I battled my way onto a BVC. I struggled a bit there, but, again, I just worked harder. I found the applications for pupillage really difficult – writing has never been a strength of mine and the questions were really demanding. I wasn't offered one interview and I eventually realised that it wasn't going to happen. They wanted achievement, not just effort, and there was nothing in my background to make me stand out.

At first I was pretty bitter, especially after spending all that money. But I had been warned of the difficulties and I hadn't really believed them. I thought that motivation and dedication would get me through, but it wasn't enough. I suppose the writing was on the wall when I couldn't get to grips with the OLPAS form. With hindsight, if I couldn't deal with that, I had little chance of success as a barrister.

I'm a bit disillusioned with law, but I know I have learned a lot and my skills are marketable. I'm much more confident now because of my advocacy training. I'm going to look for work beyond the law – I gave it my best shot and it wasn't sufficient, so I'll move on. I'm looking for a graduate traineeship with a big firm or for an entry into management consultancy.

Two very different stories – but they prove that there is life outside the law!

CHAPTER 14

Retraining as a lawyer

THE LURE OF THE LAW

If you already have a job but your ambition is to retrain as a lawyer you could be joining a significant number of other people. Some use their existing professional experience to support their legal career, for example an IT expert might specialise in computer law or intellectual property. Even your hobbies may be useful – a keen yachtsman or yachtswoman might have sufficient nautical knowledge to sail ahead in maritime law, for instance.

THINK CAREFULLY

Retraining is a big step and you could be going back into student penury at a time when you have a secure job and maybe a mortgage and are developing a taste for expensive food and holidays. Lifestyle differences can also put a strain on relationships.

If you are moving from a responsible professional position you could find starting at the bottom with a legal career very difficult.

On the plus side, after several years of full-time work your time management skills should be well developed and you should be able to cope with a full-time postgraduate course without difficulty.

WHAT SORT OF FACTORS SHOULD YOU TAKE INTO ACCOUNT IF YOU ARE CONSIDERING SWITCHING TO LAW?

HOW AND WHERE TO STUDY

Part-time study certainly eases the financial burden of retraining although it can make for some long days and nights. If you are working in a busy job from 9–5, then taking classes at night and/or at the weekends may not be very tempting. But if you are sufficiently well motivated, law degrees are available through part-time study and so are legal vocational qualifications although not all colleges offering legal courses run these part-time (see Chapter 5). Distance learning is another possibility, particularly if there is no suitable college or university close to home. This is very flexible, but it does, again, mean giving up your free time and being very self-disciplined.

Whatever you choose, any part-time programme will mean quite a lengthy period of study – say five years if you do a part-time law degree and two years or more for a conversion course such as the GDL or for a vocational scheme like the BVC or LPC.

MONEY MATTERS

On the other hand, full-time study means giving up your well-paid position. Yes, scholarships and bursaries are available (see Chapter 11), but plenty of other people will be scrambling for this sort of funding.

Some other possibilities for supporting yourself:

- discussing with your partner whether you could live on one salary for some years

- moving back into the family home if you are single (and your family agrees!)

- taking in a lodger if you have your own place

- finding a less pressurised job for a few days a week to keep yourself solvent

- doing your current work on a part-time basis and dispensing with some luxuries (such as a holiday!).

DO YOU HAVE THE RIGHT QUALIFICATIONS?

Many employers are keen to recruit more mature people – but they are not going to make any concessions in terms of the usual academic requirements that they would want from any intending lawyer. You will still need strong grades at A level or its equivalent, a good class of degree and adequate results on any vocational courses.

What if you left school without A levels etc? You may not need to retake these. You could instead go for an access course in law.

Another popular method for mature entrants is by the ILEX route (see Chapter 5).

WHAT SORT OF FIRM DO YOU WANT TO WORK FOR?

If you are aiming at one of the very top firms, such as Amelia Gould did (page 120 below), remember that they are all located in London and a few other major cities. Are you prepared to uproot if necessary? Do you have the requisite academic achievements – they will expect these no matter what your age? How much have you found out about other kinds of legal practice and local opportunities?

HOW WILL YOU OBTAIN THE NECESSARY WORK EXPERIENCE?

Again, this is non-negotiable. It's pointless saying that you don't have the time as you are already working. You will be expected to make time – perhaps by volunteering in the evenings or by using your annual leave to do some placements or shadowing.

WHAT IS YOUR FAMILY SITUATION?

If you have young children, for instance, and hope to be based in one of the most prestigious law firms, how will the hours that you will have to work impact on your domestic life? Should you be thinking of a medium-sized firm or local chain or a high-street practice instead? Civil service legal departments, local authorities and the CPS/COPFS all offer flexible work arrangements whenever possible. In all these cases, the hours can still be long at times, but not on such a regular basis. If these alternatives aren't for you and you still want to aim for the big names, what support systems – such as nannies, help from relatives – do you have?

HOW WILL EMPLOYERS VIEW YOU?

The answer to this is, generally, very favourably as long as you meet all the above criteria. One human resources officer pointed out that often the barriers don't come from the employers' side; it's the mature students themselves who lack the confidence to apply. So go for it!

WHAT DO YOU HAVE GOING IN YOUR FAVOUR?

- **Life experience** – you can probably deal with many situations that would tax a 22-year-old.

- **Business awareness** – most people who have held down a responsible job understand the commercial imperative and this is one thing that most recruiters find lacking in very young graduates.

- **Social skills** – you may find it easier to negotiate or placate difficult clients, to adopt new tactics if they are resisting your advice or to work with them on a day-to-day footing. Another feature that firms often find lacking in the younger age group is the ability to make small talk!

- **Contacts** – you will have friends or friends of friends who are already working in law. Use these to start building up a network, to find out more about the different roles and specialist areas, maybe even to gain experience.

WHAT MIGHT COUNT AGAINST YOU?

- Any perceived lack of adaptability in your approach to the job or to your colleagues.

- Any resentment at doing routine tasks while on placement or in training.

- Any unwillingness to take direction from colleagues who are more senior in status but junior in years

- Your own self-doubts!

If you can demonstrate on paper and in person that you don't possess these fatal flaws, the battle's half-won already!

As we've seen from Bridget's story at the beginning of this book (see Case Study 1, page 3), your previous career can work for you.

Case Study 15
Tom Webb was a surveyor but had always hankered after a job as a solicitor.

I made the decision to retrain and took the CPE part time. I found it heavy going, combined with a demanding job. My wife and I agreed to take a huge cut in income and that enabled me to do the LPC full-time. Before I left my old company and once I had given in my notice, I spent time with the lawyers that they used and they, in turn, introduced me to other people in the profession. I did some work shadowing and kept in touch with all my new contacts and one of them offered me a training contract. I think part of the equation was that I could bring in new clients from my past life. It all seems very easy, but really it's all about networking as well as getting the qualifications.

Case Study 16
Liz Foster wasn't so lucky. An ex-teacher, she found it hard to get a toehold in law at first.

I used my school holidays to do some placements – I was terrified of bumping into one of my pupils on work experience! Academically I was fine with both the CPE and the vocational course, but I didn't want to specialise in anything to do with education – not that there is much call for that sort of work – so it was difficult to put a positive spin on my past career. Then one of my tutors suggested that I used the fact that I had taken an active part in union affairs as a marketing ploy. The skills I'd learned there – such as negotiation and advocacy – were directly applicable. I think that's what got me a pupillage. I would say that it's up to the individual to work out what can be used as a selling point.

FINDING TRAINING PLACES

Some firms actively welcome mature entrants because they bring with them energy and commitment. Nonetheless, and despite the Age Discrimination Act, some application forms are still geared to 21-year-olds. At 30-plus you may find yourself not only asked for your A level grades but also to list positions of responsibility held in the sixth form!

Amelia's experience (Case Study 17) shows that, with persistence, training places can be found. A positive note on which to end!

Case Study 17
Amelia Gould is a trainee solicitor with Addleshaw Goddard, a Manchester firm.

I have an English degree and was a journalist. I changed to law because my next step was either a move to London or retraining. I'd studied a small amount of media law as a trainee journalist and enjoyed it. Also, as a reporter I'd spent a lot of time at the Crown Court and found it fascinating.

It was a big step. I studied at Manchester Metropolitan University for my CPE and LPC so I didn't move house. I sold my car, which wasn't too drastic as the local transport system is good.

What was strange was suddenly having to count every penny. I worked as a legal secretary in the holidays, which was quite well paid, and I did some freelance journalism work, but it was still tough.

I applied for a couple of training contracts before starting on the CPE course and did get second interviews, but at that point my knowledge of law was very limited and I wasn't offered a contract. Between my CPE and LPC years I did a work placement with a legal firm and was offered a training contract. However, I opted for a training contract with my present firm. I had worked there as a legal secretary and been very impressed. I was given a training contract and sponsorship for my LPC year.

My advice to someone thinking of retraining? Don't do it lightly. Get yourself some work experience and try to find some sponsorship. The CPE and the LPC courses are fairly demanding, but if you're prepared to work then you should pass the courses without too much difficulty.

Useful addresses

LEGAL INSTITUTIONS

Bar Council
289–293 High Holborn
London WC1V 7HZ
Tel: 020 7242 0082
Website: www.barcouncil.org.uk

Bar Library (formerly the Bar Council of Northern Ireland)
Courts of Justice
91 Chichester Street
Belfast BT1 3JQ
Website: www.barlibrary.com

Faculty of Advocates
Parliament House
Edinburgh EH1 1RF
Tel: 0131 226 5071
Website: www.advocates.org.uk

INNS OF COURT

Honourable Society of Gray's Inn
8 South Square
London WC1R 5ET
Tel: 020 7458 7800
Website: www.graysinn.org.uk

Honourable Society of the Inner Temple
London EC4Y 7HL
Tel: 020 7797 8250
Website: www.innertemple.org.uk

Honourable Society of Lincoln's Inn
Lincoln's Inn
London WC2A 3TL
Tel: 020 7405 1393
Website: www.lincolnsinn.org.uk
Email: mail@lincolnsinn.org.uk

Middle Temple
Middle Temple Lane
London EC4Y 9AT
Tel: 020 7429 4800
Website: www.middletemple.org.uk

PROFESSIONAL ORGANISATIONS

Institute of Legal Executives
Kempston Manor
Kempston
Bedford MK42 7AB
Tel: 01234 841000
Website: www.ilex.org.uk
Email: info@ilex.org.uk

Institute of Paralegals
Second Floor
Berkley Square House
Berkley Square
London W1J 6BD
Website: www.instituteofparalegals.org
Email: office@Instituteofparalegals.org

Institute of Professional Legal Studies
Queen's University Belfast
10 Lennoxvale
Belfast BT9 5BY
Tel: 028 9097 5567
Website: www.qub.ac.uk/ipls
Email: ipls@qub.ac.uk

Law Society of England and Wales
The Law Society's Hall
113 Chancery Lane
London WC2A 1PL
Tel: 020 7242 1222
Website: www.lawsociety.org.uk

Law Society Office in Wales
Capital Tower
Greyfriars Rd
Cardiff CF10 3AG
Tel: 029 2062 5254
Email: wales@lawsociety.org.uk

Law Society of Northern Ireland
Law Society House
98 Victoria Street
Belfast BT1 3JZ
Tel: 028 9023 1614
Website: www.lawsoc-ni.org
Email: info@lawsoc-ni.org

Law Society of Scotland
26 Drumsheugh Gardens
Edinburgh EH3 7YR
Tel: 0131 226 7411
Website: www.lawscot.org.uk
Email: lawscot@lawscot.org.uk

Legal Action Group
242 Pentonville Road
London N1 9UN
Tel: 020 7833 2931
Website: www.lag.org.uk
Email: lag@lag.org.uk

Notaries Society
PO Box 226
Melton
Woodbridge IP12 1WX
Website:www.thenotariessociety.org.uk
Email: admin@thenotariessociety.org.uk

Scottish Paralegals Association
Website: www.scottishparalegal.org.uk

Solicitors Regulation Authority
The Law Society's Hall
Ipsley Court
Berrington Close
Redditch B98 0TD
Tel: 0870 606 2555
Website: www.sra.org.uk
Email: contactcentre@sra.org.uk

OFFSHORE LAW SOCIETIES
Guernsey Bar
Website: www.guernseybar.com

Isle of Man Law Society
Website: www.iomlawsociety.co.iom

Jersey Law Society
Website: www.jerseylawsociety.je

APPLICATIONS

CPE Central Applications Board
PO Box 84
Guildford GU3 1YX
Tel: 01483 451080
Website: www.lawcabs.ac.uk

LPC Central Applications Board
PO Box 84
Guildford GU3 1YX
Tel: 01483 301282
Website: www.lawcabs.ac.uk

RECRUITMENT

Crown Office and Procurator Fiscal Service
25 Chambers Street
Edinburgh EH1 1LA
Tel: 0131 226 4069
Website: www.copfs.gov.uk

Crown Prosecution Service
50 Ludgate Hill
London EC4M 7EX
Tel: 020 7796 8000
Website: www.cps.gov.uk
Email: recruitment@cps.gsi.gov.uk

Public Appointments Unit
The Scottish Executive
S1 Spur
Saughton House
Edinburgh EH11 3XD
Tel: 0131 244 3033
Website: www.scotland.gov.uk/government/careers

GLS (Government Legal Service) Trainee Recruitment Team
Chancery House
53–64 Chancery Lane
London WC2A 1HS
Tel: 020 7649 6023
Website: www.gls.gov.uk
Email: glstrainee@tmpw.co.uk

FUNDING: LOANS, GRANTS AND BURSARIES

Barclays Bank
Information line: 0800 400100
Website: www.barclays.co.uk

Co-operative Bank
Tel: 0161 947 7180
Website: www.co-operativebank.co.uk

Educational Grants Advisory Service (EGAS)
501–505 Kingsland Road
London E8 4AU
Tel: 020 7254 6251
Website: www.egas-online.org.uk

HSBC
Tel: 0800 520 420
Website: www.hsbc.co.uk
Apply online at http://talkingmoneyhsbc.co.uk
(Application forms available at all branches – for specific queries go
    to website or helpline.)

Lloyds TSB
Website: www.lloydstsb.com/loansgraduate_loan.asp

Nat West Bank
Tel: 0800 761 033
Website: www.natwest.com

National Union of Students
461 Holloway Road
London N7 6LJ
Tel: 020 7272 8900
Website: www.nus.org.uk
Email: nusuk@nus.org.uk

Royal Bank of Scotland
Tel: 0131 523 2631
Website: www.rbs.co.uk

ACCOUNTANCY

Association of Chartered Certified Accountants
29 Lincoln's Inn Fields
London WC2A 3EE
Tel: 020 7059 5000
Website: www.accaglobal.com
Email: info@accaglobal.com

Institute of Chartered Accountants in England and Wales
Chartered Accountants Hall
PO Box 433
London EC3P 2BJ
Tel: 020 7920 8100
Website: www.icaew.co.uk/careers
Email: studentsupport@icaew.com

Institute of Chartered Accountants of Scotland
Student Education Department
CA House
21 Haymarket Yards
Edinburgh EH12 5BH
Tel: 0131 347 0100
Website: www.icas.org.uk
Email: enquiries@icas.org.uk

ADMINISTRATION

Institute of Chartered Secretaries and Administrators
16 Park Crescent
London W1B 1AH
Tel: 020 7580 4741
Website: www.icsa.org.uk
Email: info@icsa.co.uk

BANKING

Chartered Institute of Bankers of Scotland
Drumsheugh House
38B Drumsheugh Gardens
Edinburgh EH3 7SW
Tel: 0131 473 7777
Website: www.ciobs.org.uk
Email: info@ciobs.org.uk

Institute of Financial Services
IFS House
4–9 Burgate Lane
Canterbury CT1 2XJ
Tel: 01227 818609
Website: www.ifslearning.com
Email: customerservices@ifslearning.com

CIVIL SERVICE

Website: www.careers.civil-service.gov.uk

INFORMATION TECHNOLOGY

British Computer Society
First Floor Block D
North Star House
North Star Avenue
Swindon SN2 1FA
Tel: 0845 300 4417
Website: www.bcs.org
Email: bcshq@hq.bcs.org.uk

E-Skills UK
1 Castle Lane
London SW1E 6DR
Tel: 020 7963 8920
Website: www.e-skills.com
Email: info@e-skills.com

INSURANCE

British Insurance Brokers Association
14 Bevis Marks
London EC3A 7NT
Tel: 0870 950 1790
Website: www.biba.org.uk
Email: enquiries@biba.org.uk

Chartered Insurance Institute
42–48 High Road
London E18 2JP
Tel: 020 8989 8464
Website: www.cii.co.uk
Email: customer.serv@cii.co.uk

JOURNALISM

Broadcast Journalism Training Council
18 Millers Close
Rippingale
Nr Bourne PE10 0TH
Tel: 01778 440025
Website: www.bjtc.org.uk
Email: sec@bjtc.org.uk

National Council for the Training of Journalists
The New Granary
Station Road
Newport
Saffron Waldon CB11 3PL
Tel: 01799 544014
Website: www.nctj.com
Email: info@nctj.com

LIBRARY AND INFORMATION MANAGEMENT

ASLIB (Association for Information Management)
Holywell Centre
1 Phipp Street
London EC2A 4PS
Tel: 020 7613 3031
Website: www.aslib.com
Email: aslib@aslib.com

Chartered Institute of Library and Information Professionals
7 Ridgmount Street
London WC1E 7AE
Tel: 020 7255 0500
Website: www.cilip.org.uk
Email: info@cilip.org.uk

PATENT ATTORNEYS

Chartered Institute of Patent Attorneys
95 Chancery Lane
London WC2A 1DT
Website: www.cipa.org.uk
Email: mail@cipa.org.uk

PERSONNEL AND HUMAN RESOURCE MANAGEMENT

Chartered Institute of Personnel and Development
151 The Broadway
London SW19 1JQ
Website: www.cipd.co.uk
Email: cipd@cipd.co.uk

POLICE

Police Service in England and Wales
Website: www.policecouldyou.co.uk

Police Service of Northern Ireland
Website: www.psni.police.uk
Email: info@psni.pnn.police.uk

Scottish Police College
Tulliallan Castle
Kincardine
Alloa FK10 4BE
Tel: 01259 73 2000
Website: www.tulliallan.police.uk

PROBATION SERVICE

National Association of Probation Officers
4 Chivalry Road
London SW11 1HT
Website: www.napo.org.uk

National Probation Service
NOMS Probation
1st Floor Abell House
John Islip Street
London SW1P 4LH
Website: www.probation.homeoffice.gov.uk

Probation Training Unit
Mitre House
231–237 Borough High Street
London SE1 1JD
Tel: 020 7740 8500
Website: www.probationlondon.org.uk

PUBLISHING

London College of Communication
London SE1 6SB
Tel: 020 7514 6500
Website: www.lcc.arts.ac.uk
Email: info@lcc.arts.ac.uk

Publishing Training Centre
Book House
45 East Hill
London SW18 2QZ
Tel: 020 8874 2718
Website: www.train4publishing.co.uk
Email: publishingtraining@bookhouse.co.uk

SOCIAL WORK

Care Council for Wales/Cygnor Gofal Cymru
6th Floor
Southgate House
Wood Street
Cardiff CF10 1EW
Tel: 029 2022 6257
Website: www.ccwales.org.uk
Email: info@ccwales.org.uk

General Social Care Council
Goldings House
2 Hays Lane
London SE1 2HB
Tel: 020 7397 5100
Website: www.gscc.org.uk

Northern Ireland Social Care Council
7th Floor
Millennium House
19–25 Great Victoria Street
Belfast BT2 7AQ
Tel: 028 9041 7600
Website: www.niscc.info
Email: info@nisocialcarecouncil.org.uk

Scottish Social Services Council
Compass House
11 Riverside Drive
Dundee DD1 4NY
Tel: 0845 603 0891
Website: www.sssc.uk.com
Email: enquiries@sssc.uk.com

THE STOCK EXCHANGE

Financial Services Authority
25 The North Colonnade
Canary Wharf
London E14 5HS
Tel: 020 7066 1000
Website: www.fsa.gov.uk

London Stock Exchange
10 Paternoster Square
London ECM 7LS
Tel: 020 7797 1000
Website: www.londonstockexchange.com
Email: enquiries@londonstockexchange.com